JOURNEY TOWARD JUSTICE

PERSONAL ENCOUNTERS IN THE GLOBAL SOUTH

NICHOLAS P. WOLTERSTORFF

D0144831

Baker Academic

a division of Baker Publishing Group
Grand Rapids, Michigan

Published by Baker Academic
a division of Baker Publishing Group
P.O. Box 6287, Grand Rapids, MI 49516-6287
www.bakeracademic.com

Printed in the United States of America

Library of Congress Cataloging-in-Publication Data
Wolterstorff, Nicholas.
    Journey toward justice : personal encounters in the global south / Nicholas Wolterstorff.
        p.   cm. — (Turning south: Christian scholars in an age of world Christianity)
    Includes bibliographical references and index.
    ISBN 978-0-8010-4845-6 (pbk.)
    1. Christianity and justice. 2. Christianity—21st century. I. Title.
BR115.J8W647 2013
270.8′3—dc23   2013017836

In keeping with biblical principles of creation stewardship, Baker Publishing Group advocates the responsible use of our natural resources. As a member of the Green Press Initiative, our company uses recycled paper when possible. The text paper of this book is composed in part of post-consumer waste.

13   14   15   16   17   18   19   7   6   5   4   3   2   1

"Nick Wolterstorff is one of my 'heroes of the faith'—not just because he is a brilliant philosopher (although he is that), and not just because he is a careful and attentive reader of Scripture (although he is that too), but because he is an advocate for justice. His concern with justice is a lived concern, not just a theoretical one. His encounters with people who had been treated unjustly decisively shaped his life and re-formed both his analysis of the concept of justice and his reading of Scripture. I hope this book is widely read. It just may prompt others to listen both to the oppressed and to God—and to hunger for justice."

—**Allen Verhey**, Duke Divinity School

"Nicholas Wolterstorff has earned our respect and stirred our minds in his long career as a Christian philosopher. He has demanded our attention and struck our conscience in his more recent turn to the theory and practice of justice. Here he captures our imaginations and moves our souls as he tells the story of his journey toward justice—a journey that leads him from wisdom to witness."

—**Samuel Wells**, vicar, St. Martin-in-the-Fields, Trafalgar Square; King's College, London, England

"Ideas have consequences, the philosophers tell us. And they are right. But every idea also has a story. This is the tale of how one of American Christianity's most careful thinkers got justice deep down in his soul. *Journey toward Justice* is nothing if it is not clear. But it is more: by telling the story of how people suffering injustice touched him, Wolterstorff has also made his case deeply compelling. I put this book alongside *Lament for a Son* as his best writing for the church."

—**Jonathan Wilson-Hartgrove**, author of *Strangers at My Door*

"Nicholas Wolterstorff here explores various ways we humans have come to think about issues of justice. But rather than offer us an anatomy of viewpoints, he asks himself and us what might move us from worldview to engagement. And what moved this philosopher accustomed to canvassing and assessing 'theories' was encountering those suffering the throes of injustice yet enduring them with hope, including black South Africans, Palestinians, and Hondurans—as well as those from the societies dominating them who had come to stand with them. Here is a philosophical inquiry that is imbued with life."

—**David Burrell**, CSC, University of Notre Dame

TURNING ◆

TURNING SOUTH:

CHRISTIAN SCHOLARS IN AN AGE
OF WORLD CHRISTIANITY

Joel Carpenter, *series editor*

The Turning South: Christian Scholars in an Age of World Christianity series offers reflections by eminent Christian scholars who have turned their attention and commitments toward the global South and East. In order to inspire and move the rising generation of Christian scholars in the Northern Hemisphere to engage the thought world and issues of the global South more vigorously, the series books highlight such reorientations and ask what the implications of "turning South" are for Christian thought and creativity in a variety of cultural fields.

Contents

Series Preface

Nearly forty years ago, the Scottish church historian Andrew F. Walls predicted that Africa would become the new Christian heartland and that other regions to the global South and East would become the new main places in the world for Christian practice and thought. Few of Walls's colleagues paid him any attention then, but today we see how prophetic he was. The "coming of global Christianity," as historian Philip Jenkins put it, is gaining broad interest and attention, and its signs are quite evident. Africans have recently led the World Council of Churches and several of the Protestant world communions. The South African Nobel laureate Desmond Tutu is arguably the world's most prominent public theologian. China and Brazil are now closing in on the United States as having the world's largest national populations of Protestant Christians. And not only has the balance of Christianity's place in the world tipped markedly toward the global South and East, so has public and scholarly consciousness of it.

This global shift in Christianity's demography, vitality, and influence has caught most Christian scholars in the North Atlantic region by surprise. Their orientation and sense of mandate has been toward the problems of the increasingly post-Christian West, and their preparation for dealing with these issues has been framed within the European "Christian humanist" tradition. C. S. Lewis, Abraham Kuyper, and Dorothy Sayers are their patron saints, and one of their prime mandates has been to try to take back intellectual territory from the "cultured despisers of religion." Christian scholarly guilds, colleges, and universities are deeply oriented in this direction. Their strategies and preoccupations were forged on the anvils of European Christendom. As a result, says Walls, there is a major mismatch between Christian vigor and engagement in frontline mission and Christian resources for producing scholarly work. Christian scholarship needs a major reorientation.

Walls took that idea to heart, and he set to work rewriting the church history syllabus. It needed to reflect the implications of the gospel's traveling south and east from Jerusalem as well as to the north and west. There are others too who have been reorienting their personal and scholarly callings, and the purpose of this series is to give several Christian thought leaders the opportunity to share what they have been learning. May these reflections be powerfully instructive, so that many of you who read and ponder them will turn your hearts, minds, and vocations in this new direction.

Series Editor's Foreword

JOEL CARPENTER

When Bob Hosack of Baker Academic started thinking with me about a "Turning South" series, we decided that we would look for Christian thinkers from North America (and perhaps from Europe too) who had experienced a change of heart, mind, and professional direction because of their encounters with people from Africa, Asia, or Latin America and their ideas and concerns. If Christian intellectuals are supposed to be helping the church do its most demanding thinking about its mission to the world, then they should be ready and willing to engage the problems and issues that arise at the front lines of the church's work. Given the seismic shift of Christian vigor and activity toward the global South and East, shouldn't Christian thinkers be devoting the greater share of their time and talent to those regions too? Needless to say, the trends of Christian thought lag far behind the dramatic shift of the church's main arenas. So we have been looking for some exemplary Christian scholars who have experienced a reorientation of their calling and who are willing to tell the story of their turnabout.

The very first person who came to mind was Nicholas Wolterstorff, one of the most eminent philosophers of our time. Nick has earned great respect for his work in epistemology and the philosophy of religion, but he has a remarkable range of interests and achievements across the various "applied" fields of philosophizing—in aesthetics, ethics, politics, and education—as well as in the more purely theoretical fields of inquiry. Anyone who is acquainted with his speaking and publishing, however, sees a persistent strain in his thinking over the past thirty years: Nick cares deeply about justice. In recent years his writing has trended even more pointedly in that direction. In *Justice: Rights and Wrongs* (Princeton, 2008), Nick argues that justice comes from the recognition of basic human rights, and that these rights derive from the dignity of persons who are made in God's image. *Justice in Love* (Eerdmans, 2011) insists that justice and love are not in tension but are perfectly compatible. So where does Nick's passion for justice come from? And why has he taken it upon himself as a philosopher to make these arguments about the nature of justice?

The answer, he says, is that he encountered people who were being wronged, and he felt a deep empathy for their plight. Empathy is what gives the struggle for justice its most powerful motivation—not duty, or obligation, or any virtue one might possess, but personal knowledge or understanding of how it feels to be treated unjustly. Some people might experience empathy from their armchair reading, he says, but it comes to us most powerfully when we are confronted by the faces and the voices of those who are vulnerable and who suffer injustice.[1]

So here we have Nick's story—how he met and was confronted, head-on, by the injustices experienced by black South Africans, by Palestinian refugees, and by plain and poor folk in Honduras. He recounts that at first, these experiences affected his life "after hours," but it wasn't long before they began to affect his thinking as a philosopher too. While many, if not most, in his profession who look at justice want to ground it in a rightly ordered society, Nick said that

---

1. He tries these thoughts out first in "How Social Justice Got to Me and Why It Never Left," *Journal of the American Academy of Religion* 76, no. 3 (2008): 664–79.

his experiences taught him to ground it in the worth and dignity of persons. And while many modern Christian thinkers want to distinguish between Old Testament justice and New Testament love, Nick says that this is a false dichotomy. Christians cannot be the people of love in any consistent way without the great passion for justice that the Bible shows as coming from the living God. These matters too have been certified to him by the teaching and witness of global South Christians. If we turn in their direction, he says, we will hear the voices and see the faces of those who have been wronged. Nick's turning South changed him, fundamentally. Who knows what God might have in store for you?

Preface

Had it not been for prodding by others, I would not have written this book. This is a story. I am a philosopher. Philosophers seldom tell stories; we deal in abstractions.

Not only is it a story; it's a personal story, the story of how I came to think about justice and to think about it as I do. What I wrote at the beginning of an essay that I was invited to submit to *The Christian Century* for its series "How My Mind Has Changed" remains true:

> Autobiography does not come easy to me. I grew up in a community of Dutch Reformed immigrants in a tiny farming village in southwest Minnesota. The ethos of the Dutch Reformed was never to call attention to yourself, to be modest in all things, never to brag or boast, never to toot your own horn. If you have done something well, let others say so; don't say it yourself. The Minnesota ethos was always to understate. If someone compliments you for some fine job you have done, either say "Thanks" and let it go at that or say "Yeah, not bad I suppose."[1]

Autobiography grows poorly in such soil.

The person who prodded me the most insistently was Joel Carpenter, head of the Nagle Institute for the Study of World Christianity

---

1. *The Christian Century* 126, no. 24, December 1, 2009, 26–30.

at Calvin College. Joel had the idea of a series of books to be called "Turning South." He was aware of the fact that it was certain experiences I had in the global South that prompted me to think and write about justice as I do. So he encouraged me to write a book for his series in which I told the story of how that had gone. I use the term "global South" a bit loosely, to include the Middle East.

So that's what this book is—an autobiographical tour through my thoughts about justice rather than a systematic tour, which is the form that almost all of my previous writings on justice have taken. What I say here concerning the righting of injustice goes beyond what I have previously published; but for the rest, it's an autobiographical tour through much of the same material that I have presented systematically elsewhere. Some passages have even been lifted out of what I wrote previously, usually with some tweaking.

The fact that the material is organized in an overall narrative rather than systematic form puts things in a distinctly different light; I hope that even those readers who have read my systematic discussions of justice will find it both interesting and illuminating to have the material presented in this light. I myself found it interesting and illuminating. I saw some things more clearly than I did before; I saw connections that I had not seen before.

Judging that some readers would also find it valuable to have the "essence" of my thoughts on these matters without all the details, I decided to eschew the philosophical intricacies of my systematic treatment of the issues. I daresay that there will be other readers who are disappointed on this account—readers who find the discussion too superficial, too lacking in philosophical depth and finesse for their taste. I refer those readers to my earlier systematic treatments of the topics.

I was first awakened from my oblivion to justice—my "slumber," one might call it—by my encounter in South Africa in 1975 with Afrikaners and people of color; I was further awakened by my encounter with Palestinians in 1978. Those encounters have looming importance in the narrative that follows. So here, before the narrative begins, I want to do what I can to forestall two false impressions that readers might get. One false impression is that, in 1975, all Afrikaners were defenders of apartheid. They were not. Among them were also vocal and heroic opponents. I got to know a few of them on that first trip; I got to know a good many others later. Another false impression is that all Israelis were and are defenders of Israel's treatment of the Palestinians. They were not and they are not; a good many Israelis were and are vocal and heroic opponents of Israel's policies. I got to know a fair number of them after my initial encounter with the Palestinians.

Most of the chapters are brief: just one topic per chapter. I have grouped them into six sections. In part 1, "Awakening," I describe how I came to think about justice and how I came to think about it as I do. In part 2, "Justice and Rights," I briefly rehearse the theory of justice that I have developed more elaborately in my earlier writings on justice. Since I hold that justice is grounded in rights, I explain what I take rights to be. In part 3, "Justice in Scripture," I show how deeply embedded justice is in Christian Scripture, New Testament as well as Old Testament. In part 4, "Righting Injustice," I reflect on various dimensions of the struggle to right injustice and why it is that that struggle is typically so difficult and contentious. It was not until a visit to Honduras, just a few years ago, that I saw, with a clarity that had previously eluded me, that fundamental or "primary" justice, as I call it, is impossible in the absence of just punishment. So that is the topic of part 5, "Just Punishment." Finally, in part 6, "Beauty, Hope, and Justice," I reflect on the relation between justice and beauty and on the relation between justice and hope. I conclude with a brief recap.

Unless I indicate otherwise, my quotations from Scripture are from the Revised Standard Version (RSV).

PART 1

AWAKENING

❖ 1 ❖

Two Awakening Experiences

In September 1975, I was sent by the college at which I was teaching, Calvin College, to an international conference on Christian higher education organized by the University of Potchefstroom in Potchefstroom, South Africa, a small city located about an hour's drive from Johannesburg. At that time the university deliberately and explicitly located itself within the Afrikaner tradition. Whites who were not Afrikaners were admitted as students; but so-called blacks and coloreds were not.[1] This was the first time I had set foot in the global South.

Most of the South African scholars present at the conference were Afrikaners; but there were some so-called blacks and coloreds as well. In addition, there were scholars from other parts of Africa, a sizable contingent from the Netherlands, a number of us from North America, and some from Asian countries.

Though the conference was not about the South African system of apartheid—1975 was well before the revolution in South Africa—apartheid was the dominant topic of conversation during coffee breaks

1. The Afrikaners gave the name "coloreds" to those who had both African and white ancestors.

and meals, and constantly threatened to intrude into the conference itself. Eventually it did, first into a scheduled session of the conference, and then into a hastily called unscheduled session. The discussion in that unscheduled session was more intense than anything I had ever experienced. The Dutch were very well informed about South Africa and very angry about apartheid; they vented their anger at the Afrikaners. The Afrikaner defenders of apartheid in turn vented their anger at the Dutch. Later I would learn that Afrikaners fended off most critics of apartheid by telling them that they were misinformed. They could not charge the Dutch with being misinformed. So instead they charged them with being self-righteously judgmental. Eventually the so-called black and colored scholars from South Africa began to speak up, more in tones of hurt than of anger—or so it seemed to me at the time. They described the daily indignities heaped upon them and the many ways in which they were demeaned; they spoke of being expelled from their homes and herded off into Bantustans. With great passion they cried out for justice.

Not only was I profoundly moved by this cry for justice, I felt convinced that I had been issued a call from God. I did not hear words in the air; it was by way of the speech of the so-called blacks and coloreds that God spoke to me. Fidelity to God required that I speak up for these victims of injustice in whatever way might prove appropriate.

While in South Africa, I learned of the existence of its antiterrorism laws. These allowed the police to detain a person for ninety days without filing a public charge, without notifying anyone where the person was held, without giving the person access to an attorney, and with the right to renew the ninety-day period repeatedly if they so wished.

Before going to South Africa I had known of the heroic resistance to apartheid by C. F. Beyers Naudé, a member of one of the prominent old Afrikaner families. For me it was a matter of conscience to have an interview with Naudé while in South Africa; so it was arranged that, after the conference was over, I, along with Gerald Vande Zande from Canada, would have an interview with Naudé in our hotel in Pretoria. The interview was never held. Two days before, one of Naudé's principal assistants had been arrested under the antiterrorism detention laws; Naudé was so preoccupied with reorganizing his staff and trying to find out where his assistant was being held that he had to break the appointment.

Deeply disturbed over the existence of a society in which such an arrest could take place, I walked the streets of Pretoria that night with a professor from Malawi who had attended the conference, venting my anger. After some thirty minutes, I noticed that my companion was absorbing all this with little noticeable reaction. I asked him how it could be that if I was so angry, he could be so calm. I shall never forget his answer: "I live with this sort of thing every day of my life. If ever I would criticize my government outside a tiny circle of trusted friends, I would be arrested, my family would lose its means of livelihood, and my seminary would be closed down." I saw more vividly than ever before what a privilege it is to live in a country where I can vigorously criticize my government in public without fearing reprisal.

Upon returning home I bought yards of books about the situation in South Africa and its historical origins, and read avidly. I began to think, speak, and write about justice in general and about injustice in South Africa in particular. I returned to South Africa a number of times and became friends with many opponents of the old regime— black, colored, and white. Of these, it was Allan Boesak who became one of my dearest friends and who, over the years, has remained that through thick and thin.

In May 1978, I attended a conference on Palestinian rights on the west side of Chicago. I do not know why I was invited, nor have I ever understood what it was in myself that impelled me to attend. The conference was sponsored by an organization called the Palestine Human Rights Campaign. There were about 150 Palestinians present, mostly Christian; they poured out their guts in flaming rhetoric, rhetoric too hot, I later learned, for most Americans to handle. They described the indignities daily heaped upon them. They told of how their ancestral lands and orchards were being confiscated and of how they were evicted from their homes and their homes bulldozed to make room for Jewish settlers. They told of collective punishment and of the multiple ways in which they were daily demeaned. They cried out with great passion for justice. I was deeply moved by the cry. And again I felt convinced that I had been issued a call from God to speak up for these wronged people in whatever way might prove appropriate.

The US State Department had allowed Ambassador Terzi, who at the time was the Palestinian Liberation Organization (PLO) representative to the United Nations, to attend the conference on the condition that he see to it that whenever he spoke, there be no more than five people within earshot. This infuriated me. If my country's policy in the Middle East was so fragile that it would be endangered by more than five people simultaneously hearing what Terzi was saying, then there must be something profoundly wrong with the policy.

Upon returning home I bought yards of books about the situation in the Middle East and its historical origins, and read avidly. I spoke and wrote about injustice in the Middle East. I became chair of the board of the Palestine Human Rights Campaign, and organized and spoke at conferences that the Campaign sponsored. I traveled to the Middle East several times, and became friends with a number of those who were protesting the situation, both Israeli and Palestinian. When the Oslo Accord was signed on September 13, 1993, I concluded that the situation was now in the hands of the Israelis and the Palestinians and that there was little that foreigners like myself could now contribute. How naive!

Why were these two experiences so moving for me? I had been a vocal supporter of the American civil rights movement, though I had not traveled to the US South to participate in protest marches. I had been a vocal opponent of the Vietnam War; I had spoken out publicly in opposition. Rereading some of the things I wrote at the time, I notice that the basic moral categories that I employed for thinking and speaking about these situations were those of justice and injustice.

But I had not felt called, not in the way I did when confronted by the situations in South Africa and Palestine. I had not been motivated to think, speak, and write about justice.

John Rawls's now-classic text *A Theory of Justice* was published in 1971.[2] The acclaim and attention it immediately received led me to read it soon after it appeared, more out of intellectual curiosity than anything else, since political philosophy and ethics were not among my specialties in philosophy (I never taught a course or seminar in either until after I retired). I found Rawls's book intellectually intriguing and some of the discussions surrounding it fascinating. But I was not moved to think for myself about justice, nor was I motivated to read further in the literature on justice.

So why was my response so different when I heard the so-called blacks and coloreds in Potchefstroom cry out for justice, and why was it so different when I heard the Palestinians gathered on the west side of Chicago cry out for justice?

I think it was because in Potchefstroom, and on the west side of Chicago, I was face-to-face with the wronged. I was not reading what someone had written about some abstract thing called justice, but neither was I reading newspaper reports about the victims of injustice somewhere. I was listening to live human beings telling their own stories of how they and their families and friends were systematically demeaned and humiliated. As they told their stories, I fastened on their faces, looked into their eyes, absorbed their words. Nothing of this sort had happened to me before. The injustices with which I had been personally acquainted were mainly episodes. These people were not speaking about episodes in their lives; they were describing the daily condition of their existence.

They, the wronged, came to me; I had not gone out looking for them. When I went to Potchefstroom, I expected a leisurely discussion on Christian higher education. I do not know what I was expecting when I went to the conference on Palestinian rights, but certainly not

2. John Rawls, *A Theory of Justice* (Cambridge, MA: Harvard University Press, 1971). A revised edition was published by Harvard University Press in 1999.

that I would be confronted by 150 Palestinians crying out for justice. In both cases, I was overtaken.

Not only was my thinking, writing, and speaking about justice motivated by seeing the faces and hearing the voices of people who were systemically wronged; their contours have been shaped by that starting point.

In *A Theory of Justice* John Rawls did not start from the wronged; he started from various problems in political and ethical theory. The same is true for that enormous body of writing that was spurred by Rawls's publication; it is by professors and for professors, about issues that professors find intellectually intriguing. I too am a professor, a professor of philosophy. But my experience in Potchefstroom in 1975 and on the west side of Chicago in 1978 made it impossible for me not to start from the wronged in my reflections on justice.

The response to the "blacks" and "coloreds" by the Afrikaners at the conference who spoke up in defense of apartheid took me completely aback. They did not contest the charge of injustice; but neither did they concede the charge and resolve to join the oppressed in the struggle to right injustice. They insisted that justice was not a relevant category. Order and disorder were the relevant categories; South Africa was threatened with disorder. And as to the whole project of apartheid, they insisted that this was an act of goodwill on the part of the ruling Afrikaners. In South Africa, they explained, there were some ten or eleven different nationalities. The system of apartheid was inspired by the ideal of each of these nationalities finding its own cultural identity. If that was to happen, they could not live mingled among one another; they would have to live separately, apart—hence, *apartheid*.

To this, some added stories about their own individual acts of charity: clothes they gave to the "black" family living in the backyard that their own children had outgrown, trinkets that they gave to the family at Christmas, and so forth. Some of my fellow North Americans were skeptical of these stories; I was not.

In short, they, the Afrikaners, presented themselves as a benevolent people. They complained that so often their benevolence went unacknowledged; no gratitude was forthcoming. Why can't we just love each other, one of them asked plaintively of the "blacks" and the "coloreds"; why do you only criticize us? And they complained that critics of apartheid ignored the visionary beneficent ideal that motivated the project; the critics only took note of the difficulties encountered in achieving the ideal.

What I saw before my eyes, as I had never seen before, was benevolence being used as an instrument of oppression—*self-perceived* benevolence, of course.

Why was it so important to the Afrikaners who spoke up in defense of apartheid at the conference that they resist thinking of the situation in terms of justice and injustice, and think of it only in terms of order and goodwill? Because for them to concede that the "blacks" and "coloreds" were being treated unjustly would require putting brakes on their own passion for order and on their self-perceived paternalistic benevolence; it would require advocating the rejection of the whole project of apartheid. And that was something they could not bring themselves to do. Not only were they inspired by the great good that apartheid would supposedly yield, they were satisfied with their own position in the situation; they were calling the shots and living comfortably. Of course, they did not themselves make this last point, that they were calling the shots and living comfortably.

What is it about justice that puts brakes on paternalistic benevolence? And why, more generally, does justice matter? Why are goodwill and benevolence not enough? At the time I had no answers to these questions. Now I think I do. We'll be getting to them later.

And why did the Afrikaners who spoke up at the conference in defense of apartheid not respond to the cry for justice as I did? Not only was I emotionally moved, I felt that I had been issued a call from God to speak up for these wronged people. The Afrikaners responded instead by arguing that justice was not a relevant category. Yet at the conference they were face-to-face with the same "blacks" and "coloreds" that I was face-to-face with; in their daily lives they were face-to-face with many more. They heard the same human beings telling the same stories of humiliation and demeaning that I heard. They looked into those same eyes—or maybe not, maybe they didn't look into their eyes. But they saw the same faces. Why did they respond with cool argumentation, and with the aggrieved claim that they felt hurt because their benevolence was so seldom recognized and acknowledged with gratitude? At the time I also had no answers to these questions; some hunches, but no more than that. Now I think I do have some answers. We'll also be getting to those later.

❖ 2 ❖

An Evening in Amman

Four years after my encounter with the Palestinians in Chicago, my wife, Claire, and I visited the Middle East, with stops in Lebanon, Jordan, Israel, and the occupied West Bank. In Israel and the West Bank we talked at length with both Palestinians and Israelis. Following is a slightly revised version of what I wrote, upon our return, about one of our experiences.[1]

Father Iliya Khoury is a Palestinian Arab. Born and reared in the West Bank, he is now in his sixties, I would judge, and is the assistant bishop in the Jerusalem diocese of the Anglican Church. My wife and I met him in Amman, Jordan, however—not in Jerusalem. Some years ago the Israeli authorities imprisoned Fr. Khoury for eight months (two of them in solitary confinement) and then, without granting him a hearing, expelled him from Israel. He had been too outspoken in condemning the injustices being wreaked on his people. Now, in exile, he is serving a small congregation of Palestinians in Amman.

No doubt many North Americans think of all Palestinians as

1. Published in *The Reformed Journal* 32, no. 7 (July 1982); reprinted in my *Hearing the Call* (Grand Rapids: Eerdmans, 2011).

11

Muslims—and fanatical. Indeed, we tend to think of the entire Middle East, apart from some outposts in Jerusalem and Bethlehem, as empty of Christians except for a few struggling groups established by Protestant missionaries early in this century. The truth is that this is where the Christian church began and where it has never died out. Here are to be found the most ancient churches in all of Christendom. There has always been a Christian presence in the Middle East, and not just in the places of pilgrimage. What makes us overlook these our brothers and sisters in Christ?

My wife and I were part of a group of Americans who visited the Middle East this spring, not vacationing but attempting as Christians to understand the situation of the church there and the conflict of peoples and religions. In Lebanon we talked to the head of the Maronite Church, the head of the Armenian Church, a bishop of the Melkite Church, and representatives of the Middle East Council of Churches; we also spoke with Muslims, and with representatives of the Lebanese government, of the PLO, of the rightist Falangist Party, and of the Syrian Nationalist Party. During a stay of a few days in Jordan, en route to Israel, a friend of ours said to us, "You must meet Fr. Khoury." Although a meeting with our entire group could not be arranged, my wife and I were offered the opportunity to talk with Fr. Khoury. We met in a small room on the bottom floor of what appeared to be a sort of home and parish house combined.

Let me present to you Fr. Khoury's witness. I cannot convey the blend of sorrow, hope, and passion with which he spoke; I can only give his words. I did not take notes while he was speaking. But as soon as we got back to our hotel I jotted some things down. That was hardly necessary. His words were unforgettable.

Why, he asked, has the world church abandoned us Christians here in the Middle East? We are deserted, forgotten by the church of the whole world. Why? Why do Christians in America support the Zionists instead of supporting us, their brothers and sisters in Christ? I do not understand. They do not even notice us. We are abandoned. Perhaps we Palestinians have not known how to cry out.

We are caught between the Israelis and the Muslims. The Muslims see Western Christendom as behind Israel. They see Israel as an outpost of the West—of the *Christian* West. They want no part of it. I tell you, they are becoming fanatics, worse than at any time in my memory. If things continue as they are, we will become martyrs. We are willing to become martyrs if that is demanded of us. We shall remain faithful. But you are forcing us to become martyrs in an unworthy cause.

My people, my Christian people, are being destroyed, squeezed between Israel and the Muslims. A few years back, 12.5 percent of the Palestinians were Christian; now only 6 percent are. We are constantly shrinking, constantly getting smaller. What has happened? Have the people abandoned Christ? Have they converted to Islam or Judaism? No, they have not. They are being forced out of Israel by its Zionist policies. Israel is destroying the church in Palestine. Soon, in the land of our Lord, there will be no Christians left. The old ones have their homes taken from them by the Israelis, confiscated. The young ones, seeing no future, leave for the United States, for South America, anywhere. Why do Christians in America support the Zionists when they are destroying the church in Palestine? Why do they not support their brothers and sisters in Christ?

I am told that conservative Christian groups in the United States are planning to start a radio station aimed at the Muslims. Why do they not first speak to us about such things? Why do they ignore us? Why do they act as if there are no Christians here? We have lived with the Muslims for more than a thousand years. Why do they not first ask our advice? They say that we have not been successful in evangelizing the Muslims. What do all your Western missionaries have to show for their efforts? I tell you, this will only make Muslims more nervous, more suspicious, more fanatical. Our oppression will become worse. It would be easier to convert the devil himself at this point than to convert a Muslim. Today they are not receptive. You will cause Christianity to disappear from the Middle East unless you stop this American style of evangelism and unless your government settles the Palestinian issue.

I operate a small school here in Amman. Both Christians and Muslims come to the school. I do not try to convert the Muslim children. I try to show them that Christians and Muslims can live together in peace. Unless the Muslims believe that, and unless the Zionists cease their oppression, the church here in the Middle East will disappear.

What I need for my own congregation is a small place where we can meet during the week. My people must meet so that we can support each other in these difficult days. But we have no money. So I went to Europe to ask the Christians there for money. Do you know what they told me? They told me that *they* had decided that it was unwise for the church to spend money on buildings!

Why do the churches in the rest of the world not trust us? Instead of piping in their Western evangelism, why do they not support us in building meeting places for our people, and schools, and in holding discussions between Christians and Muslims so that we can learn to live together? Believe me: I love Jesus Christ. I love the gospel. I speak from the standpoint of that love. I say: trust us. Do not compete with us. Support us. We know the Muslims. We live with them.

Eventually Israel will see that the Palestinians are its only door to the Arab world. It will see that its only hope is to form a society in which Jews, Muslims, and Christians live together. The first step to such a society will be a Palestinian state on the West Bank and in Gaza, with East Jerusalem as its capital. But that will not happen unless you Americans help to settle the Palestinian issue—until you see the justice of our cause. You are driving the Palestinians into the arms of the Russians, where we do not want to be. And you are destroying the church.

God will not desert us. And we will not desert God. Perhaps I sound despairing. But I am not. I live in the hope that our Lord will come. But how much must we suffer? Help us, before it is too late. Unless the baby in its crib cries out, no one pays attention. Perhaps we have not known how to cry out.

Please convey this to my Christian brothers and sisters in America. You may use my name.

❖ 3 ❖

Questions about Starting
from the Wronged

hy did you have to go abroad for your awakening?" some readers will ask. I mentioned that though I had been a vocal supporter of the civil rights movement in the United States, I had not myself gone down south to participate in protest activities. Had I done so, I would almost certainly have seen the faces and heard the voices of those who were wronged by the laws and practices of racial discrimination in my own country. So why didn't I go down south? Or more pointedly: Why did I not see the faces and hear the voices of those wronged by racial discrimination and other forms of oppression in my own city of Grand Rapids, Michigan?

In Charles Dickens's novel *Bleak House* there is a character, Mrs. Jellyby, whose eyes are so fixed on suffering in distant Africa that she pays no attention to the plight of her own ill-fed, poorly clothed, untended children. This is cheap liberalism.

"Miss Ansell" was the name of an actual Mrs. Jellyby with whom I had the ill fortune to become acquainted. Miss Ansell owned a large Victorian house on the outskirts of Cambridge, England. In the fall of 1956 my wife and I rented two rooms on the second floor of her house; a young Israeli couple rented the other rooms on the floor. It was clear to us that they were very poor.

This was at the time of the Hungarian Revolution. Miss Ansell spent all day every day at her desk writing letters to world figures urging them to do something to stop the Russian invasion of Hungary. She wrote to the British prime minister offering to lay her body across the tracks of the trains transporting Russian soldiers into Hungary if the British government would pay for the cost of her travel to Hungary.

Miss Ansell had a large garden in the back of her house with a number of apple trees in it. The trees were ripe with fruit; the apples were beginning to fall. The Israeli couple asked if they could pick some of the apples. Miss Ansell tartly replied that they were not to go into the garden; the garden was off limits to her renters. Her eyes were so firmly fixed on injustice in distant Hungary that she never saw the wrong she was doing to her renters. This was cheap liberalism.

Was it not also cheap liberalism on my part to be awakened to issues of justice and injustice by the plight of the wronged in distant South Africa and in the distant Middle East? *Cheap*, because it cost me nothing to criticize what the Afrikaners were doing to people of color in South Africa or what the Israelis were doing to the Palestinians. As I would learn later, Afrikaners who criticized their government paid a high cost, as did those Israelis who criticized the policies of their government. On one occasion, when we had a visiting Afrikaner over to our house for dinner, the name of Beyers Naudé came up. After listening for a while he said, with great intensity, "Beyers is a traitor." Was the fact that my awakening occurred abroad and not at home due, perhaps, to a subconscious awareness that being awakened to systemic injustices at home would cost me something?

I do not defend how things went in my life; I only describe. I did not set out looking for victims of systemic injustice. Perhaps I should have, but I did not. They came to me, unexpectedly. And I had no doubt that, by way of their cries, God had called me to speak up for these wronged people. It would have been religiously and morally irresponsible for me not to do so—irresponsible to declare that I had other priorities.

But was I not belittling them in taking it on myself to speak up for them? Was I not guilty of the very paternalism that I attributed to the Afrikaners? Were these people not capable of speaking up for themselves? Should I not have encouraged them to do so, and should I not have supported them when they did? Or if for some reason they were not capable of speaking up for themselves, should I not have worked to empower them so that they became capable?

They did speak up for themselves. The people of color at the conference in Potchefstroom spoke up for themselves; the Palestinians at the conference on the west side of Chicago spoke up for themselves. I did not shunt them aside and take over. In saying that I felt called to speak up for them, what I mean is that I felt called to stand alongside them as they spoke up for themselves. I did not see that, and do not see that, as belittling them. I see it as honoring them.

The criticisms I have mentioned to my starting from the wronged whom I encountered are moral objections. I imagine another objection of quite a different sort; it's an objection to anybody starting from *any* wronged, not just to *my* starting from *these* wronged.

Not only did my encounter with the wronged in South Africa and the Middle East motivate me to think, speak, and write about justice, it also motivated me to think, speak, and write about justice from a particular standpoint—namely, the standpoint of one who, though not himself systemically wronged, found himself empathetically united with some who were.

The objection is that thinking about justice from such a standpoint intrudes bias into one's reflections, especially when those reflections are intertwined with advocacy for the wronged. There's nothing wrong with advocacy as such. But the philosopher, so some say, has an obligation to be objective by standing above the fray and describing for us how things look from nowhere in particular.

Late in his life the great German sociologist Max Weber gave a lecture that he entitled "*Wissenschaft als Beruf*," perhaps best translated as "Academic Work as Calling."[1] In his lecture Weber rehearsed his theory of modernization as it applies to the academic disciplines. In modernized societies, the sphere of academic work has been differentiated from other spheres of human activity and has become autonomous, freed from external influences and freed for the pursuit of its own distinct values in accord with its own unique dynamics. Academic freedom is the combination of this freedom from and freedom for.

The autonomy of the sphere of academic learning is not, however, a once-for-all achievement; in certain times and places it is threatened. Near the end of his lecture, Weber launched an almost bitter attack on those who use their professorial position as a platform for advocating one or another cause. Advocacy has no place in the university; it is an alien, distorting intrusion. The obligation of the scholar in the modern world is to resist such intrusion and stick to following the internal dynamics of his or her academic discipline. Here is part of what Weber said:

> Science [academic learning] today is a "vocation" organized in special disciplines in the service of self-clarification and knowledge of inter-related facts. It is not the gift of grace of seers and prophets dispensing sacred values and revelations, nor does it partake of the contemplation of sages and philosophers about the meaning of the universe. This . . . is the inescapable condition of our historical situation. We cannot evade it.

Some, especially among the young, continue to yearn for a prophet.

> [But] you will certainly not compel him [a prophet] to appear on this earth by having thousands of professors, as privileged hirelings of the state, attempt as petty prophets in their lecture-rooms to take over his role. All they will accomplish is to show that they are unaware of the decisive state of affairs: the prophet for whom so many of our younger generation yearn simply does not exist.

1. The lecture is to be found in H. H. Gerth and C. Wright Mills, *From Max Weber: Essays in Sociology* (New York: Oxford University Press, 1946).

Any professor who aims to gratify the yearnings of the young by using the lecture room as a pulpit is a false prophet. The "inward interest" of a true prophet "is not served by veiling from him and others the fundamental fact, that he is destined to live in a godless and prophetless time, by giving him the *ersatz* of armchair prophecy. The integrity of his religious sensibility must rebel against this."[2]

Over the past forty years, political philosophy in the American academic world has mainly been a series of glosses on Rawls, glosses on glosses on Rawls, and so forth. The critic I am imagining says that I should have thought about justice from the standpoint of a participant in that discussion. Rather than thinking about justice from the standpoint of someone who is empathetically united with people who were systemically wronged, I should have thought about justice from the standpoint of a philosopher engaged with other philosophers in thinking about justice. When viewed from that standpoint, what I have written about justice looks strange and distorted. The philosophical issues that I take up and emphasize are distinctly different from those taken up and emphasized by other philosophers writing about justice; worse yet, I have allowed myself to wander into areas outside my competence as a philosopher: intellectual history, sociology, theology, biblical interpretation.

My response is that to think about justice from the standpoint of a university professor, who is neither himself systemically wronged nor empathetically identified with those who are, is not to think about justice from *no* standpoint; it is to think about justice from *that* standpoint.

The question that preoccupied Rawls in his late writings was how a liberal democracy could be stable and just when its citizens adhere to a variety of comprehensive religious and philosophical doctrines or perspectives. His answer to that question came in the form of a theory as to how citizens of well-formed liberal democracies should reason with one another. The fact that this question preoccupied

2. The quoted passages come from ibid., 152–53. I have slightly revised the translation.

Rawls is to be attributed, in good part, to the internal dynamics of the discipline of political philosophy; Weber was right in holding that there are such dynamics. But there was more to it than that. It also reflected the particular standpoint that Rawls occupied in thinking about justice. The question that preoccupied him was not a question that preoccupied people of color in South Africa or the Palestinians in the Middle East.

Those of us who engage philosophical issues have no choice but to do so from whatever standpoint we find ourselves occupying. There is, for us, no God's-eye point of view; we articulate how things look from where we stand. We do so, however, while listening carefully and responsively to whatever serious objections are raised by those who view things from a different standpoint. In some of my writings I have called this way of engaging in philosophy *dialogic pluralism*.

Fair enough, it may be said. Anyone who engages in philosophy or any other academic discipline does so from a certain standpoint; nobody ever does so from nowhere. But in seeing myself not only as theorizing from the standpoint of someone who was empathetically identified with the wronged whom I had encountered, but also as *speaking up* for them, was I not doing what Weber found so reprehensible—namely, inserting politics into the academy, mixing advocacy with reflection?

In my writings I have indeed expressed the view that the people of color in South Africa and the Palestinians in the Middle East were being systemically wronged; thereby I was speaking up for them. It was obvious to me from the beginning that those judgments were controversial. But how is one to develop a theory of justice if one has no prior convictions as to what is just and what is unjust against which to test one's theory?

Someone might reply by conceding the point, but then go on to add that one should confine oneself to testing one's theory against those cases of justice and injustice that everyone agrees on—for example, that torture as a means of punishment is wrong.

But if the theory someone arrives at when appealing only to such cases has the implication that apartheid was not a violation of justice, I will conclude that there is something wrong with the theory. Conversely, if it has the implication that apartheid was a violation of justice, the Afrikaners at the conference who spoke up in defense of apartheid would have concluded that there was something wrong with the theory. We who are theorists cannot escape disagreement on such matters. We cannot avoid speaking up.

❖ 4 ❖

One Difference That Starting from the Wronged Made

What difference does it make if one starts from the wronged? Or better: What difference did it make for *me* that I started from my empathetic identification with *these* wronged people?

Let me begin my answer to this question by distinguishing between two forms of justice; one I will call *primary* justice, the other, *reactive* justice. Let me first explain reactive justice.

When one is wronged one acquires certain rights that previously one did not have, the right, for example, to be angry at the person who did the wronging, sometimes the right to punish that person or to support that person's being punished by the state or some other institution, and so forth. One is now *permitted* to be angry at the wrongdoer, *permitted* to punish or support punishment. Call these *permission-rights*.

Some of the things one is permitted to do on account of having been wronged are sometimes things one *ought* to do. In some cases, for example, one is not just permitted to punish or support the punishment of the wrongdoer but obligated to do so. One owes it to the members of one's community to see to it that the wrongdoer is punished so that he does not repeat his wrongdoing. If so, then the members of one's community have a *claim* or a *right* to one's punishing or supporting the punishment of the wrongdoer; they have what can be called a *claim-right* to one's doing that. If one tried to prevent punishment of the wrongdoer one would wrong the members of one's community, fail to treat them as they have a right to be treated, fail to honor the legitimate claim they have to one's punishing or supporting the punishment of the wrongdoer. (In a later chapter I will have a good deal more to say about the connections I am assuming here among obligations, permission-rights, and claim-rights.)

Let me henceforth call the complex of permission-rights and claim-rights that are acquired by virtue of someone wronging someone *reactive* rights; the idea behind calling them this is that they are rights acquired *in reaction* to being wronged. And let me call all other rights *primary* rights. One's right not to be insulted by the receptionist in the health clinic is a primary right; it's not a right that one acquired by being wronged. Reactive rights are the rights acquired by a violation of primary rights.

Corresponding to reactive rights is *reactive justice*; corresponding to primary rights is *primary justice*. Later we will be discussing in some detail the connection between justice and rights.

I did not hear the cry for justice by the people of color in South Africa and by the Palestinians as a cry for reactive justice; I did not hear them crying out for punishment of wrongdoers. I'm sure they believed that a good many people should be punished for what they were doing; but I did not hear their cry as a cry for that. After the fall of the apartheid regime there was a great deal of discussion in South Africa concerning a particular form of reactive justice—namely, what has come to be called *transitional justice*—justice in the transition from a massively unjust regime to a just regime. Much of this discussion has focused on the work of South Africa's Truth and Reconciliation Commission.[1] But in 1975, the fall of the apartheid regime and the

---

1. A good recent discussion of transitional justice is Daniel Philpott, *Just and Unjust Peace: An Ethic of Political Reconciliation* (New York: Oxford University Press, 2012).

formation of the Truth and Reconciliation Commission were both still well in the future.

I heard the cry for justice by the people of color in South Africa and by the Palestinians as a cry for *primary* justice. I think it was because, in their cry for justice, I did not hear a cry for reactive justice but instead a cry for primary justice that in my thinking, speaking, and writing about justice I concentrated for a long time on primary justice. It was not until a much later experience in Honduras that I was impelled to think about reactive justice.

It took me some time to realize—now it seems obvious—that the cry for primary justice by the people of color in South Africa and by the Palestinians had two dimensions: it was simultaneously a cry for the doing of primary justice and a cry for the cessation of primary injustice and the undoing of its effects. For the sake of brevity, let me call this latter cry a cry for *the righting of primary injustice*. The cry I heard was a cry for the doing of primary justice and a cry for the righting of primary injustice. It's important to keep both of these dimensions in mind.

In the opening pages of *A Theory of Justice*, John Rawls describes his project in the book as formulating the principles of social justice for a well-ordered society.[2] He explains that by "principles of social justice" he means principles that "provide a way of assigning rights and duties in the basic institutions of society and . . . define the appropriate distribution of the benefits and burdens of social cooperation."[3] And he explains that by "a well-ordered society" he means "a society in which (1) everyone accepts and knows that the others accept the same principles of justice, and (2) the basic social institutions generally satisfy and are generally known to satisfy these principles."[4]

2. John Rawls, *A Theory of Justice*, rev. ed. (Cambridge, MA: Harvard University Press, 1999). The quotations and pagination will be from this edition.
3. Ibid., 4.
4. Ibid. In *Political Liberalism* (New York: Columbia University Press, 1993), Rawls's position is that a well-ordered society need not have one shared conception of justice but may have a certain shared family of conceptions.

Having explained what he means by "a well-ordered society," Rawls immediately goes on to observe that

> existing societies are of course seldom well-ordered in this sense, for what is just and unjust is usually in dispute. Men disagree about which principles should define the basic terms of their association. Yet we may still say, despite this disagreement, that they each have a conception of justice. That is, they understand the need for, and they are prepared to affirm, a characteristic set of principles for assigning basic rights and duties and for determining what they take to be the proper distribution of the benefits and burdens of social cooperation.[5]

Rawls's thought here is that our actual societies fall short of being well ordered because, though most of us see the need for a just assignment of rights and duties, benefits and burdens, we have serious disagreements concerning the principles for the assignment.

Shortly after he makes this point it becomes clear that Rawls thinks that existing societies fall short of being well ordered in a way that is even more fundamental. To his initial explanation of a well-ordered society he adds, a few pages later, that in a well-ordered society "everyone is presumed to act justly and to do his part in upholding just institutions."[6] But in existing societies, citizens do not all act justly and do not all do their part in upholding just institutions; far from it. Thereby our actual societies fall well short of being well ordered.

Rawls says that a theory of justice for our existing societies—he calls such a theory a "partial compliance theory"—would have to treat "such topics as the theory of punishment, the doctrine of just war, and the justification of the various ways of opposing unjust regimes, ranging from civil disobedience and conscientious objection to militant resistance and revolution." It would have to treat "questions of compensatory justice and of weighing one form of institutional injustice against another."[7] Such questions, Rawls says,

5. Rawls, *Theory of Justice*, 5.
6. Ibid., 8.
7. Ibid.

are "the pressing and urgent matters. These are the things we are faced with in everyday life."[8]

If these are "the pressing and urgent matters" of everyday life, why does Rawls not deal with them? The reason he gives for dealing instead with ideal theory is "that it provides . . . the only basis for the systematic grasp of these more pressing problems. . . . At least, I shall assume that a deeper understanding can be gained in no other way, and that the nature and aims of a perfectly just society is the fundamental part of the theory of justice."[9] Rawls never got around to addressing the more "pressing and urgent matters" of everyday life in any systematic way.

The picture one gets from these passages is that the way to get a complete theory of justice for our actual societies is to combine a theory of justice for ideal societies with a theory of reactive justice—justice in punishment, justice in warfare, justice in opposition to unjust regimes, and so forth. I regard this as seriously mistaken.

If one starts from the wronged in developing a theory of primary justice, one obviously does not rest content with developing ideal theory; that is to say, one does not rest content with developing principles for the distribution of rights and duties, benefits and burdens, by the basic social institutions of a society in which everybody is treated justly and everybody agrees on the principles of justice. But neither does one simply clamp onto ideal theory a theory of reactive justice. Let me explain why.

First, primary justice and injustice in society are not confined to how the basic social institutions of that society distribute rights and duties, benefits and burdens. There is also justice and injustice in interpersonal relationships. The indignities that the so-called blacks and coloreds in South Africa experienced were by no means limited to their treatment at the hand of the state and other basic social institutions. Knowing how the basic social institutions of one's society should distribute rights and duties, benefits and burdens, does not tell us what constitutes justice in our interpersonal relationships.

8. Ibid.
9. Ibid.

Second, suppose that for some reason we decide to concentrate our attention on how rights and duties, benefits and burdens, are distributed by the basic social institutions of society. From the fact that certain principles would yield justice of distribution by the basic social institutions in a well-ordered society, it does not follow that those same principles would yield justice of distribution by those institutions in our actual societies. In our actual societies some people are greedy and some are not, some are devious and some are not, some are self-centered and some are not, some are lovers of wealth and some are not, some have few moral scruples and some are deeply conscientious, some feel empathy with the downtrodden and some do not, some are reasonable in how they debate political issues with their fellow citizens and some are not. A legislator in one of our actual societies, when trying to craft just laws, has to take account of these wide differences in disposition; a philosopher crafting laws for a well-ordered society does not.

Starting from the wronged implies that, in developing a theory of primary justice, we will aim at a theory that applies not only to the basic institutions of society but applies to our interpersonal engagements as well. And it implies that the principles we arrive at for the just distribution of rights and duties, benefits and burdens, by the basic institutions of society will be principles of distribution for this actual world of ours, not principles for an imagined ideal world.

Twenty-two years after the publication of *A Theory of Justice*, Rawls published *Political Liberalism*. In the years that intervened between the publication of the two books he came to a somewhat different understanding of a well-ordered society. He came to think that, in the modern world, a well-ordered society that is a liberal democracy will be a society in which citizens embrace a diversity of reasonable comprehensive doctrines, religious and otherwise, many of which have their own distinctive way of thinking about justice. It is for this reason that the dominant question of *Political Liberalism* is how a liberal democracy can be just and stable, given that its citizens embrace a diversity of comprehensive doctrines.

There can be no doubt that this question is of fundamental importance for modern liberal democracies; I have written a good deal on the topic myself. But Rawls is no less preoccupied with ideal theory in *Political Liberalism* than he was in *A Theory of Justice*. The difference is that he came to think of the well-ordered society somewhat differently. He still does not start from the wronged—no more than in *A Theory of Justice*.

Depending on how a particular liberal democracy deals with the issue of religious diversity, there may well be citizens of that polity who are treated unjustly on account of their religion. If so, they are wronged. One's reflections on primary justice might start from them. More generally, one's reflections on primary justice might start from any of those many people around the globe who are wronged on account of their religion. My reflections started not from people who were wronged on account of their religion but from people who were wronged by apartheid and by the insistence of the Israelis that Israel be a Jewish state and that it not give up its occupation of the West Bank.

In *The Republic* Plato developed a theory of justice for an ideal society; Rawls followed in Plato's path. Starting from the wronged meant that I would have to tread a different path.

❖ 5 ❖

Another Difference
That Starting
from the Wronged Made

What difference did it make, I asked, that my reflections on justice started from the wronged whom I encountered in Potchefstroom in 1975 and on the west side of Chicago in 1978? The answer to this question that I gave in the preceding chapter was that starting from the wronged meant that I could not follow in the tradition, stretching from Plato to Rawls, of developing a theory of primary justice for an ideal world.

It made another difference as well. In my reflections on primary justice, I eventually came to see that there are two fundamentally different ways in which we in the West think about justice. These two ways of thinking are operative both in theorists and in laypeople. I call one of these ways of thinking the *right order* conception of justice; I call the other the *inherent rights* conception. The fact that my reflections on justice started from the wronged led me, almost ineluctably, to the inherent rights conception. Let me explain why, starting with an explanation of the difference between the two conceptions.

The right order theorist holds that a society is just insofar as it is rightly ordered, and he or she holds that a society is rightly ordered insofar as the members of society conform their actions to some objective standard. Different right order theorists hold different views as to the nature of that objective standard. John Rawls is a right order theorist who held that the objective standard consists of principles that the members of society have fairly agreed on for the distribution of rights and duties, benefits and burdens, by their basic social institutions. Catholic right order theorists typically hold that the objective standard is natural law. For Plato it consists of the abstract form or idea that he called *justice itself*, or sometimes *the just thing itself*. The contemporary theologian Joan Lockwood O'Donovan holds that it consists of what she calls "the objective matrix of obligations."[1]

To get hold of the basic idea, let's work with O'Donovan's way of thinking. What she calls the "objective matrix of obligations" consists of abstract generalities; it tells us how X-type people in X-type situations are obligated to treat Y-type people in Y-type situations. For example, it tells us that X-type people in X-type situations are obligated to help Y-type people in Y-type situations cross the street. If I then happen to be an X-type person in an X-type situation, and you happen to be a Y-type person in a Y-type situation, I am obligated to help you cross the street.

Some writers call this obligation that I have, to help you cross the street, a *subjective* obligation, on the ground that it attaches to a subject, in this case, to me. I *have* that obligation, I *possess* that obligation.

And what about rights on this way of thinking about justice? Some right order theorists reject all thought and talk about rights; in subsequent chapters I will have something to say on why that is. Others are willing to think and talk about so-called *positive rights*—rights that are conferred on us by legislation or social practice, or generated

1. See her essay "The Concept of Rights in Christian Moral Discourse," in Michael Cromartie, ed., *A Preserving Grace: Protestants, Catholics, and Natural Law* (Grand Rapids: Eerdmans, 1997), 143–56.

in us by a speech act such as promising—but only about positive rights. This is the position of Joan Lockwood O'Donovan, as it is of her husband, Oliver O'Donovan. Oliver O'Donovan puts it like this:

> The language of subjective rights [i.e., rights that adhere to a particular subject] has, of course, a perfectly appropriate and necessary place within a discourse founded on law. One's "right" is the claim on which the law entitles one to demand performance. . . . What is distinctive about the modern conception of rights, however, is that subjective rights are taken to be original, not derived. . . . The right is a primitive endowment of power with which the subject first engages in society, not an enhancement which accrues to the subject from an ordered and politically formed society.[2]

I hold that anyone who thinks of the objective standard as an objective matrix of obligations should accept not only positive rights but also natural rights; her position implies their existence. Here's why. She will of course hold that there are natural subjective obligations—that is, obligations possessed by particular persons, particular subjects. These are the obligations that we have by virtue of the objective matrix applying to us. But if I have a natural subjective obligation to help you cross the street, then you have the correlative natural right to my helping you cross the street. Your right to my helping you is the correlative of my obligation to help you.

For the purpose of understanding the right order theory, the important point to notice about this natural right that you have is the following: my being an X-type person in an X-type situation, and you being a Y-type person in a Y-type situation, is not sufficient for you to have a right to my helping you cross the street. In addition, there has to be that objective matrix that *bestows* on me the obligation to help you cross the street, given that I fit the X-type slot and that you fit the Y-type slot. The converse side of that objective matrix bestowing that obligation on me is then your right to my helping you cross the

2. Oliver O'Donovan, *The Desire of the Nations* (Cambridge: Cambridge University Press, 1996), 262.

street. Obligations are directly bestowed, and their correlative rights
are then indirectly bestowed.

That was the right order conception of justice. Now for the inherent rights conception. The inherent rights conception says that
there is something about each human being, and something about
her relationship to her fellows, that gives her rights; there doesn't have
to be, in addition, some external standard bestowing rights on her.
There is something about you, and something about our relationship
to each other, that gives you a right to my helping you cross the street.
Your right to my doing so is *inherent* in something about you and our
relationship to each other; it's not added on.

The inherent rights theorist, then, holds that justice is present in
society insofar as people are treated as they have a right to be treated.
Obviously the big challenge facing the person who thinks about primary justice along these lines is to identify what it is about persons
and human beings, and about their relationship to each other, that
gives them rights. We'll be getting to that in later chapters.[3]

Here is the core of the difference between the two conceptions.
Right order theorists have their eyes on some objective standard—be
it Platonic forms, natural law, an objective matrix of obligations, just
principles of distribution justly arrived at, or whatever—and they
hold that society is just insofar as people conform to that standard.
If they believe in natural rights at all—and many, for example, the
O'Donovans, do not—they believe that they are bestowed, in some
way, by that objective standard. Inherent rights theorists have their
eyes on persons and human beings. They hold that there is something
about these, and something about their relationship to each other, that
gives them rights; and they hold that society is just insofar as persons
and human beings are treated as they have a right to be treated.

As I noted, right order theorists can, in principle, join inherent
rights theorists in holding that there are natural rights. The nub of

3. I speak of persons *and* human beings for the following reason: there are some
human beings who are so seriously impaired that they are not functioning as persons;
they are human beings but no longer persons. On the other hand, God is a person
who is not a human being.

the difference does not lie there. It lies in what one takes to be the deep structure of the moral order. Right order theories of primary justice are, as it were, top-down theories; inherent rights theories are bottom-up theories.

When I listened to the people of color in South Africa and to the Palestinians tell their stories about how they were daily humiliated and demeaned, and when I heard their cry for justice, I did not have in mind the distinction between these two ways of conceiving of justice, the right order conception versus the inherent rights conception; distinguishing them came much later. But when I did finally identify and distinguish these two ways of conceptualizing justice, it was at once clear to me why, from the very beginning of my reflections on justice, I had thought of justice in terms of the inherent rights conception. I had intuitively connected the cry of these people for justice to their stories of being humiliated and demeaned; nothing in what they said led me to connect it to whether or not their society conformed to some objective standard. In their stories they did not talk about objective standards. They spoke of how they were treated.

They were treated with indignity. Someone cannot be treated with indignity if he or she has no dignity. It was the dignity of the people of color in South Africa and the dignity of the Palestinians that was being violated. The Afrikaners paid no attention to the dignity of the people of color in South Africa; the Israelis paid no attention to the dignity of the Palestinians. That was the root of the injustice—failure to treat these human beings as befitted their dignity, not failure of society to conform to some abstract objective standard.

In issuing their call for the doing of primary justice and for the righting of primary injustice, did the people of color in South Africa and the Palestinians speak of their rights and of violations of their rights? I don't recall; if they did, it did not register with me. But they might well have done so. Other people of color in South Africa have done so, and other Palestinians have done so. Indeed, all the great social justice movements of the twentieth century employed the language of rights: those who campaigned for the abolition of child labor spoke of the rights of the child; those who campaigned for unions spoke of the rights of the laborer; those who campaigned for women's suffrage spoke of the rights of women; those who campaigned for civil rights spoke, obviously, of rights; those who campaign for the abolition of abortion speak of the rights of the unborn child. In a subsequent chapter we will see why it is that movements for social justice almost always employ the language of rights.

PART 2

JUSTICE AND RIGHTS

❖ 6 ❖

Opposition to Rights-Talk

When I began thinking, speaking, and writing about rights, I almost immediately encountered opposition, sometimes intense. Lots of people, it turns out, are hostile to rights-talk. They want to get rid of it. Why?

For a number of different reasons. Some are opposed to rights-talk for political reasons. As I observed in the preceding chapter, all the great social protest movements of the twentieth century in the West employed the language of rights. One way to defend disagreement with one or another of these social protest movements is to insist that members of the group in question do not have the rights being claimed for them. Children do not have a right to be kept out of the labor force until they are of age, women do not have a right to vote, Jews do not have a right to be treated equally in the university and elsewhere, and so forth.

But often defenders of the status quo have found the whole discourse of rights menacing; so, rather than contesting the claims being made for rights, they have tried to change the terms of the debate. Instead of talking about rights, let's talk about responsibilities, about the social bonds of friendship and loyalty, about what's necessary for a well-ordered society. That was the strategy of the Afrikaners who spoke up in defense of apartheid at the conference in Potchefstroom. We should be talking about order, they said, not about rights; we should be talking about our responsibilities to each other. Rather than the so-called blacks and coloreds insisting on their rights, we should all be asking how we can love each other.

Others oppose rights-talk because it is so often used to make inflated claims. I know someone who spent his career working for the US Centers for Disease Control who wants nothing to do with rights-talk. He is very clear on why he is opposed. Over the years he found himself repeatedly confronted by members of international health organizations couching their favorite ideals in the language of rights: people living in the tropics were said to have a right to the eradication of malaria, people living in Africa were said to have a right to the elimination of river blindness, and so forth. It seemed to him that the reason they couched their favorite ideals in the language of rights was that they could then argue that pursuit of the ideal was mandatory, not optional, thereby making those realists who claim that the ideal is at present unattainable feel guilty. He resented such manipulation, and wound up hostile to all talk about rights.

Yet another objection to rights-talk comes from those who oppose it because it is so often accompanied by what a philosopher friend of mine calls "rights absolutism." What he has in mind is the all-too-common practice of declaring that some person or group has a certain right and then refusing to discuss the matter further, brooking no disagreement, treating the claim as absolute, infallible, never allowing for the possibility that one might be mistaken.

A fourth objection to rights-talk is probably the most common of all: such talk, so it is said, is made to order for expressing and encouraging one of the most pervasive and malignant diseases of modern society—namely, the mentality of possessive individualism. It's made to order for an "entitlement society" such as ours. In using such talk, so it is said, one places oneself at the center of the moral universe, focusing on one's own entitlements to the neglect of one's obligations and to the cultivation of those virtues directed toward others that are indispensable for the flourishing of our lives together. The use of rights-talk demotes the giving self and promotes the grasping self, demotes the humble self and promotes the haughty self. It both encourages and is encouraged by the possessive individualism of the capitalist economy and the liberal polity. It invites us to think of ourselves as sovereign individuals. Rights-talk, so the objection goes, is for the purpose of *me* claiming *my possessions*, *you* claiming *your possessions*, *him* claiming *his possessions*, *her* claiming *her possessions*. That's what it's for: claiming one's possessions, giving vent to one's possessiveness, each against the other.

Joan Lockwood O'Donovan puts the point like this in one of her essays. "The modern liberal concept of rights," she says, "belongs to the socially atomistic and disintegrative philosophy of 'possessive individualism.'"[1]

> A close analysis of the history of the concept of subjective rights in the light of earlier theological-political conceptualization reveals a progressive antagonism between the older Christian tradition of political right and the newer voluntarist, individualist, and subjectivist orientation. The contrasting logic of the two orientations may be conveyed quite simply: where in the older patristic and medieval tradition, God's right established a matrix of divine, natural, and human laws or objective obligations that constituted the ordering justice of political community, in the newer tradition God's right established discrete rights, possessed by individuals originally and by communities derivatively, that determined civil order and justice.[2]

She then describes in somewhat more detail what she calls "the older traditions":

1. Joan Lockwood O'Donovan, "Natural Law and Perfect Community: Contributions of Christian Platonism to Political Theory," in *Modern Theology* 14, no. 1 (January 1998): 20.
2. Joan Lockwood O'Donovan, "The Concept of Rights in Christian Moral Discourse," in *A Preserving Grace: Protestants, Catholics, and Natural Law*, ed. Michael Cromartie (Grand Rapids: Eerdmans, 1997), 145.

In the older traditions, the central moral-political act on the part of ruler and ruled alike was to consent to the demands of justice, to the obligations inhering in communal life according to divine intention and rationally conceived as laws. The ruler commanded, legislated, and issued binding judgments, but these acts were to embody his consent to an order of right and obligations binding his own will. The subject was obligated to obey the ruler's commands, statutes, and judgments, not only because of his rightful authority, but also because these acts conformed to the requirements of justice.[3]

Given what she sees as the patent incompatibility between the idea of natural human rights and sound Christian theology, an obvious question for O'Donovan is "why Christian thinkers have been and are willing" to buy into the idea. Why have they been "willing to adopt a child of such questionable parentage as the concept of human rights"? It is, she adds, a "question that has yet to be satisfactorily answered."[4]

It seems a priori unlikely that the Palestinians and the people of color in South Africa could rightly be accused of expressing and encouraging the attitude of possessive individualism on account of their use of the language of rights in their cry for justice. At this point in our discussion, however, we should remain open to the possibility that an analysis of the concept of rights will reveal that, unwittingly, they were doing exactly that.

The question to be considered, concerning each of the objections mentioned, is whether the objection points to an avoidable abuse of rights-talk or to something intrinsic to it. An objection to rights-talk obviously carries a great deal more weight if it points to something intrinsic to such talk than if it points to an avoidable abuse.

If it points to an avoidable abuse, then the appropriate response is to note that all parts of our moral vocabulary are subject to abuse. Abuse of the language of love is all about us. The language of obligation is abused by the domineering husband who insists that his wife is obligated to obey his orders because he is "head of the household."

3. Ibid.
4. Ibid., 155.

One does not toss out some part of our moral vocabulary just because it is abused. One asks whether its abuse can be diminished, and whether something important would be lost if that part of our moral vocabulary were no longer available to us—whether something important would be lost if we could no longer talk about love, if we could no longer talk about obligation, if we could no longer talk about rights. If one judges that the abuse can be diminished and that something important would be lost if we discarded that part of our moral vocabulary, then one campaigns against the abuse and points to what would be lost. Those who oppose rights-talk seldom ask whether something important would be lost if we discarded the language of rights.

Only if we understand what rights are can we decide whether those opposed to rights-talk are pointing to avoidable abuses or to something intrinsic. And only if we understand what rights are can we discern whether something important would be lost if the language of rights and all synonyms thereof were to disappear from our moral vocabulary. So that's what I turn to next. What are rights?

❖ 7 ❖

What Are Rights?

A well-known formula for justice handed down to us from antiquity comes from the ancient Roman jurist Ulpian: justice, said Ulpian, is rendering to each his or her *ius*—that is, his or her right, his or her due. Ulpian's formula is a definition of just action: to act justly is to render to each his or her right. Justice characterizes our relationships when we render to others what is their right. It seems likely that Ulpian intended his formula to apply both to what I am calling *primary* justice and to what I am calling *reactive* justice. For some time yet in this essay, my attention will be focused on primary justice. And until we get to reactive justice, it will be claim-rights that we are concerned with, not permission-rights.

Notice that Ulpian is tacitly distinguishing between having a right and being rendered that right—or as I will sometimes say, *enjoying* that right. Not being rendered one's right not to be insulted does not mean that one does not then have that right. It means that one is not enjoying this right that one has, that one is not being rendered this right. If one has a certain right, then one may either be rendered that right or not be rendered it. If one is not, one is wronged. Being wronged is the dark side of having a right, just as guilt is the dark side of obligation. The person who is not rendered what she has a right to is wronged; the person who does not do what she ought to do is guilty.

It is sometimes thought that to have a right consists of standing in the relation of having (possession) to some metaphysically mysterious entity called "a right." This is then made the basis of an objection to rights; there are no such metaphysically mysterious entities.

This is all wrong. One doesn't just *have a right*, period. A right is always a right *to something*. Having the right consists of standing in a certain relation *to that something*, whatever that "something" may be. It makes no sense to say that one has a certain right but that there is nothing to which one has that right. The whole term "having a right to" expresses the relation between oneself and that "something" to which one has the right. The indefinite article "a" does no work in the expression "having a right to"; one might just as well say "having right to": having right to not being insulted, for example. Compare our English expression "for the sake of." The word *the* does no work in this expression; there is no such thing as *the sake*.

The relation of having (a) right to something is a normative relation. Specifically, to stand to something in the relation of *having (a) claim-right to* it is to stand to that "something" in the normative relationship of *having (a) legitimate claim to* it. Or to express the idea in yet a third way, to have a claim-right to something is to stand to that "something" in the normative relationship of its *being due* one.

To what sort of thing can one stand in the normative relationship of having a claim-right to it? Always it is to some state or event in one's life. More specifically, it is to some state or event in one's life that would be a good in one's life, a life-good; a claim-right is never to something that would be an evil in one's life.

We can be more specific yet. The life-goods to which one has a claim-right are always *ways of being treated*. Normally it's to the good of being treated a certain way *by others*. In the limiting case, it's to the good of being treated a certain way *by oneself*. We can wrong ourselves; we do so, for example, if we allow ourselves to become drug addicts. It will simplify our discussion if we set the limiting case off to the side and say that that to which one has a claim-right is always some way of being treated by others that would be a good in one's life.

Our use of the language of rights rather often conceals from us the fact that claim-rights are legitimate claims to ways of being treated. I have a right to walk on the Charlottesville Mall. My walking on the Charlottesville Mall is not a way of being treated, however; it's something I do. To say that I have a right to do it is to say that it is something that I am permitted to do; I have a permission-right to walk on the Charlottesville Mall. But if we look a bit deeper, we see that there is also a claim-right in the region—namely, my right *to be free* to walk on the mall without hindrance. Being free to walk on the mall without hindrance is a way of being treated. So too, though taking a seat on the plane is something one does, not a way of being treated by others, and is hence a permission-right, if we look deeper we see that there is a claim-right in the region—namely, the right *to be allowed* to take a seat on the plane—and that is a way of being treated.

Earlier I said that rights are normative relationships. What we can now add is that rights are normative *social* relationships; that to which one has a claim-right is always to the good of being treated a certain way. It takes at least two to have a right—with the exception of those cases in which one has a right to being treated a certain way by oneself. Rights have sociality built into them.

If Ulpian was right—and I think he was—that justice consists of being rendered that to which one has (a) right, then what we can now say is that primary justice is present in society insofar as the members of society stand to one another in the normative social relationship of being treated as they have a right to be treated.

❖ 8 ❖

Rights Grounded in Worth

W e now confront the greatest challenge facing anyone who tries to construct a theory of rights: the challenge of explaining the nature of the normative social relation that one has to one's fellows when one *has a right* to being treated a certain way by them.

Though that to which one has a claim-right is always a way of being treated that is or would be a good in one's life, the converse is not the case: there are many ways of being treated that would be a good in one's life to which one does not have a claim-right. I think it would be a great good in my life were the Rijksmuseum in Amsterdam to give me one of their Rembrandt paintings to hang on my living room wall, along with a security force to stand guard. But I don't have a right to the museum's doing that; my not enjoying the good of the museum's treating me that way does not imply that the museum is thereby wronging me. So what accounts for the fact that, of those ways of being treated that would be a good in one's life, one has a right to some of those and not to others?

As we noted earlier, some of our rights are bestowed on us by legislation or social practice; I have a right to receive a monthly Social

Security check from the US government on account of the Social Security legislation passed in the 1930s and the fact that I possess the qualifications specified in the legislation. Others of our rights are generated in us by certain speech acts; I have a right to your doing what you promised me you would do. But not all our rights are of these sorts. Some are *natural* rights. Wholly apart from legislation, social practices, and speech acts, I have a right to not being murdered, to not being tortured for the pleasure of the torturer, to not being insulted or demeaned. So what accounts for the fact that, of those ways of being treated by others that would be a good in one's life, one has a *natural* right to some of those ways of being treated while to others one either has no right or only a socially bestowed or linguistically generated right?

The view on this matter that is presently dominant in the philosophical literature is that natural rights are to be understood as safeguards for one's fundamental natural right to personal autonomy—that is, for one's fundamental natural right to form for oneself a plan of life and to enact that plan. In his recent book *On Human Rights*, James Griffin says that we should "see human rights as protections of our normative agency."[1] It's because the exercise of normative agency has special importance that "we ring-fence [it] with the notion of human rights."[2]

Popular though this line of thought is, it won't do. One problem for the theory is explaining the concept of autonomy that is being employed. Obviously nobody has the right to do whatever he or she sees fit to do; so what, then, is that to which, supposedly, we each have a fundamental right? I judge that no theorist has succeeded in answering this question satisfactorily. If this were the only problem with the theory, I would have to defend that judgment here. But it's not.

Another problem is that if natural rights are understood as protections of our fundamental right to autonomy, then we need an account of what it is that gives us a right to autonomy. If one tries to

1. James Griffin, *On Human Rights* (Oxford: Oxford University Press, 2008), 2.
2. Ibid.

get around this by declaring that personal autonomy is a great good, but not something to which one has a right, one is then left without a theory of rights. If some way of being treated is a great good but not something to which one has a right, then whatever protects that great good is also no more than a good, not something to which one has a right. If I don't have a right to the good of being given a Rembrandt painting, then I also don't have a right to the good of a security force to stand guard.

A third problem is that a good many of our rights don't have anything to do with autonomy. To torture imprisoned criminals as a way of punishing them is to wrong them; they have a right not to be punished by torture. But what makes it wrong is not that their autonomy is thereby impaired. Their autonomy is already impaired; they are locked up. So too, I find it grotesque to say that what's wrong about rape is that the victim's autonomy is impaired. It is indeed. But is that what makes it wrong?

Here's a counterexample of a different sort: suppose that I spy on you for prurient reasons but do nothing at all with what I learn other than enjoy it in private at home. I have wronged you; you have a right not to be so spied upon. But my action has no effect whatsoever on your autonomy.

Or consider those human beings sunk deep into Alzheimer's. They have rights—for example, the right not to be shot and have their bodies tossed into a dumpster for waste management to haul away. But they are completely lacking in autonomy; they cannot engage in normative agency. Neither can those human beings in a permanent coma.

My own view is that rights are grounded in the worth, the value, the dignity of human beings. We all have worth on account of some achievement on our part, some capacity that we possess, some property that we have, some relationship in which we stand. We are all praiseworthy in various respects; we are all estimable for various reasons.

With that in mind, notice that there are ways of treating a person or human being that befit her worth and ways of treating her that do not befit her worth—ways of treating her that would only befit someone or something of lesser worth, ways of treating her that consist of treating her with disrespect or under-respect, ways of treating her that demean her. If you are a student in a philosophy course that I am teaching and you have done top-notch work in the course, then what befits your worth as someone who has done top-notch work is my giving you an A on your record.

Raping someone does indeed impair her autonomy; but what is wrong, at bottom, about rape is not that the rapist impairs the victim's autonomy but that he treats this human being as worth no more than something he can use to give him pleasure or to display his power. So too, what was wrong about putting slaves up for sale is that thereby one was profoundly demeaning those human beings, treating them as worth no more than two-legged workhorses.

Now I can say what I think rights are. Rights are ways of being treated that are required by respect for worth. You have a right to being treated a certain way by me just in case, were you not treated that way by me, you would be treated in a way that does not befit your worth, your dignity. If torturing you is incompatible with treating you as befits your dignity as a person, then you have a right not to be tortured. If putting you up on the block for sale is incompatible with treating you as befits your dignity as a person, then you have a right not to be put up on the block for sale. If my giving you anything less than an A for the course would not befit your worth as someone who has done top-notch work, then you have a right to an A from me. And so forth.

Understanding what rights are requires distinguishing between, on the one hand, how well or poorly a person's life is going—his well-being—and, on the other hand, the worth or value of that person himself. A truly admirable person may find that his life is going poorly; those are the Jobs of the world. Conversely, a person whose life is going very well may not be a very admirable person. This gives rise to the ancient complaint, why do the wicked prosper? The complaint presupposes a distinction between the worth or admirability of the person, and the worth or admirability of his life.

Rights represent the interweaving between, on the one hand, ways of being treated that would be a good in our lives, and, on the other hand, the worth that we ourselves have. The recognition of rights requires the recognition of ways of being treated that would be a good in our lives. But it requires, in addition, recognition of the worth, the dignity, the estimability of persons and human beings themselves. Any ethical theory that works only with life-goods, and not also with the worth or dignity of persons or human beings, is incapable of giving an account of natural rights. One does not get rights by piling up life-goods. On the one hand, being given a Rembrandt painting to hang on my living room wall would be a great good in my life, but I do not for that reason have a right to that good. On the other hand, receiving a pleasant response from the receptionist would be a relatively small good in my life; nonetheless, I have a right to it.

❖ 9 ❖

Why Rights-Talk Is Important

We have seen that justice is important because justice is based on rights, and rights are important; and we have seen that rights are important because one's rights are grounded in one's worth, and being treated by one's fellows as befits one's worth is important. But there are other things important about rights that we have not yet taken note of.

Suppose that the Afrikaners who spoke up in defense of apartheid at the conference in Potchefstroom had been granted their wish that nobody talked about the situation in South Africa in terms of justice and rights but only in terms of benevolence, generosity, love, charity, and the like. What would be lost? What does the language of rights enable us to do that the language of benevolence, generosity, and the like does not enable us to do?

The language of rights enables us to call attention to the wrongs wreaked by paternalistic benevolence; thereby it enables us to voice a moral brake on such benevolence. That much is already clear. But what is it about rights that give them this braking role?

In the literature on rights one finds it said that rights have "trumping force" or "peremptory force." What's meant is that if you have a right to the good of my treating you a certain way, then no matter how many good things I may bring about by not treating you that way, I ought to treat you that way. Not treating you that way is morally off the table; it's not a morally permissible option. It's the trumping force of rights that enables them to function as moral brakes on the evils of paternalistic benevolence.

Suppose, once again, that you are a student of mine who has done top-notch work in a course I am teaching; you have a right to an A. But imagine now that you are rather cocky and full of yourself; I judge that a B-minus might induce some desirable character reformation. So I give you a B-minus and highlight the flaws in your work; experienced professors can find flaws in even the best student work.

To do that would be to wrong you; you have a right to an A. And so it follows that I ought not do that. Giving you a B-minus is off the table; it's not a morally permissible option. If I think you need some character reformation, I will have to find some other way of bringing that about, a way that does not wrong you.

The example is a minor example of the general point. The twentieth century was filled with regimes that believed it was acceptable to treat some people like animals or worse if doing so would bring about the good society for others. If we cannot appeal to the rights of people, if we cannot argue that to treat human beings this way is to wrong them and is hence off the table, morally impermissible, we have no way to stop this "calculus of goods" way of thinking, this utilitarian mentality.

Let's grant, for the sake of argument, that the society the Afrikaners envisioned, in which each nationality would be segregated to find its own cultural identity, would have been a good thing. I find that dubious; but for the sake of argument, let's grant that it would have been a good thing. The massive injustices perpetrated on the so-called blacks and coloreds in the course of trying to attain that vision meant that attaining the vision in that way was morally impermissible. The benevolent impulses of the Afrikaner did not excuse the injustice. There's a lot of paternalistic benevolence in the world, much of it, though not all of it, profoundly unjust. It's because rights have trumping force that the language of rights enables us to voice a moral brake on such benevolence.

And why do rights have this peremptory or trumping force? We can see why they do by noting their connection with obligations. The connection can be formulated in a *Principle of Correlatives*, as I have called it in some of my writings. This principle says that, whoever Ruth and Mike may be, Ruth has a right to Mike's doing X if and only if Mike has an obligation toward Ruth to do X. For example, Ruth has a right to Mike's ceasing to insult her just in case Mike has an obligation toward Ruth to cease insulting her.

And now notice that if I am obligated to do something, then it is morally impermissible for me not to do it; or if I am obligated not to do something, then it is morally impermissible for me to do it. If Mike has an obligation toward Ruth to stop insulting her, then it's morally impermissible for him to insult her even if he could bring about all manner of good things by continuing to insult her.

So consider once again the cocky student. If he has a right to being given an A by me, then, by virtue of the Principle of Correlatives, I have an obligation toward him to give him an A—even if giving him a B-minus would effect a desirable character reformation. And if I have an obligation toward him to give him an A, then it is morally impermissible for me not to do so. That's why his right to being given an A trumps all the goods that might be achieved by giving him a B-minus.

This line of thought suggests the following question. I asked what would be lost if we had only the language of benevolence, love, charity, generosity, and the like available to us, and not the language of rights and wrongs. My answer was that what would be lost is our ability to voice a moral brake on paternalistic benevolence, and I argued that it is on account of the peremptory or trumping force of rights that rights-talk has this function. But my argument shows that the language of duty and obligation also has trumping force; thus it too can be used to voice a moral brake on paternalistic benevolence.

So suppose that we no longer had the language of rights and wrongs available to us, but that we still had available the language of duty and obligation. We could use the language of duty and obligation to voice a moral brake on paternalistic benevolence. So would anything then be lost? Couldn't everything that we presently do and say with the language of rights instead be done and said with the language of duty and obligation? Instead of saying that you were not treated by me as you had a right to be treated, we could say that I did not treat you as I ought to have treated you. These two ways of speaking have somewhat different rhetorical flavors. But they pick out and express the same normative relation, do they not? Same fact, different words.

The suggestion has to be rejected. Recall my declaration, when I was explaining what a right is, that a right is to the good of being treated a certain way. Notice that I used the passive voice: *being* treated a certain way. I submit that the moral order has two fundamental dimensions: the agent-dimension and the patient-dimension, the actor-dimension and the recipient-dimension. On the one hand, there is the moral significance of what one does; on the other hand, there is the moral significance of how one is done unto. On the one hand, there is the moral significance of how one treats others; on the other hand, there is the moral significance of how one is treated *by* others.

The language of rights, and its companion language of being wronged, is for bringing to speech the recipient- or patient-dimension of the moral order, the dimension of how we are done unto. In thinking about the moral order, the philosophical tradition has focused almost all of its attention on the agent-dimension. Thereby it has, in my judgment, given us a seriously incomplete and distorted picture of the moral order as a whole.

Consider an abused spouse, and suppose that the only language available to her is the agent-language of love, charity, and the like, along with the language of duty and obligation. With such language she can call attention to the moral condition of her abusive husband: he is acting unlovingly, he is guilty of not doing what he ought to do, and so forth. What she cannot do is call attention to *her own* moral condition. She has been wronged. Rights-talk enables her to call attention to that.

If talk about rights disappeared from our moral vocabulary, we would no longer have available to us the language for calling attention to the moral significance of how we and others have been done unto, the language for calling attention to the fact that someone has been wronged. The reason rights-language has almost always been the preferred language for social protest movements is that such language enables the oppressed to call attention to their own moral condition.

Let's get at this same two-dimension idea from a different angle. In the case just discussed, we noted the difference between the abused spouse having only the language of the agent-dimension available to her for describing the morality of the situation, versus having available as well the language of the patient-dimension. Now imagine that you are reflecting not on how you have been done unto but on how you yourself should treat some person or group of persons. What's the difference between thinking of the situation only in terms of the agent-dimension, and thinking of it also in terms of the patient-dimension? What's the difference between thinking of it only in terms of your duties and your generosity, and thinking of it also in terms of the rights of those others? Suppose you are a teacher. What's the difference, when you enter the classroom, between thinking of the situation wholly in terms of your duties and your generosity, and thinking of it also in terms of the rights of the students? Here is another example. What is the difference between a parent thinking of his relation to his child wholly in terms of his own duties and thinking of it in terms of the rights of the child and of the possibility that his actions may wrong the child?

Though these seem to me fundamentally different orientations, I do not find it easy to put the difference into words; but let me try. The second orientation requires that one be open to the worth of the students or the child in a way that the first does not. Thereby it requires a decentering on one's part. I place myself in the shoes of the other person or persons. I am no longer in moral control of the situation. I am, as it were, a moral listener, open to recognizing their worth and to the claims that such recognition places upon me.

The problem with the Afrikaners who defended apartheid was that they were so full of their own goodness and virtue that they never opened themselves up to recognizing the moral significance of how the so-called blacks and coloreds were being treated, never noticed the significance of how they were being done unto. The defenders of apartheid resisted moral decentering. They wanted to be in charge. They wanted their self-perceived benevolence to be received with gratitude. And they insisted that the so-called blacks and coloreds be on good behavior or the benevolence would not be forthcoming. That's how it is with benevolence. Benevolence is optional; generosity can be conditioned. The requirement that I pay due respect to you for your worth has no conditions—none at all.

Suppose that Ruth's house is south of Mike's. It makes no difference whether one uses the sentence "Ruth's house is south of Mike's" to describe the spatial relation of their houses or the sentence "Mike's house is north of Ruth's." Same fact, different words. Should the words *south of* disappear from our vocabulary, that would make no difference whatsoever to our ability to pick out and express the fact about the spatial relationship of the houses, provided that the words *north of* remained.

Rights-talk and obligations-talk are not related like that. They do not pick out the same moral facts. The Principle of Correlatives makes it tempting to think that they do, but they do not. That they do not is perhaps most clear when obligations and rights are viewed from the "shadow" side. My *being guilty* of not treating you as I ought to treat you is not the same fact as your *being wronged* by how you were treated by me.

The relation between *my having a duty* and *your having a right* is not like the relation between *being south of* and *being north of*; it's like the relation between a triangle's *being equiangular* and its *being equilateral*. A triangle is equiangular if and only if it is equilateral, necessarily so; nonetheless, these are different facts. The proposition "a triangle is equiangular if and only if it is equilateral" is what philosophers call a synthetic necessary truth, not an analytic necessary truth. So too, the Principle of Correlatives is a synthetic necessary truth. Those who deny the principle, as some do, are denying a necessary truth but not affirming a contradiction.[1]

If we no longer had the language of rights available to us, then, even if we retained the language of obligation, we would no longer be able to bring to speech the patient-dimension of the moral order. That's what would be lost.

---

1. James Griffin in *On Human Rights* (Oxford: Oxford University Press, 2008) denies the principle.

❖10❖

Is Rights-Talk for Expressing Possessive Individualism?

The language of rights enables us to give voice to the patient- or recipient-dimension of the moral order. And by virtue of the trumping force of rights, it enables us to voice a moral brake on unbridled benevolence. But what about the common charge against rights-talk, mentioned earlier, that the language of rights is for expressing the mentality of possessive individualism and that its use encourages that mentality?

When one sees things from the standpoint of someone in our entitlement-preoccupied society who is not himself systemically oppressed—from the standpoint of a white male university professor, for example—the charge may seem plausible. But when the people of color in South Africa used the language of rights in their protest against the injustice of apartheid, were they expressing the mentality of possessive individualism? Implausible on the face of it. When the Palestinians used the language of rights in their protest against the injustices inflicted on them, were they expressing the mentality of possessive individualism? Implausible. Was the civil rights movement in the United States a vast outburst of possessive individualism? Most implausible. One's standpoint makes a difference in how things look.

If a right is what I said it is—a normative social relationship, grounded in one's worth or dignity, and consisting of a legitimate claim to the life-good of being treated a certain way—then it's clear that the charge against rights-talk of expressing and abetting possessive individualism points to an abuse of the language rather than to something inherent in it. There is a normative social bond between you and me whereby you bear legitimate claims on me as to how I treat you and whereby I bear legitimate claims on you as to how you treat me. The situation is symmetrical. The language of rights is for bringing this reality to speech. The person whose mentality is that of possessive individualism will, of course, talk much about his own right to be treated in certain ways and ignore the rights of others to his treating them in certain ways. But that's an abuse of rights-talk. The culprit in the situation is not the language of rights but the mentality of possessive individualism that wrests the language of rights to its own malign purposes.

A good many writers would challenge the claim just made, that rights-talk employed as an expression of the mentality of possessive individualism is an abuse of the language. Possessive individualists are not abusing rights-talk, so these writers say; they are using it as it is meant to be used. Rights-talk carries possessive individualism in its DNA.

Those who hold this view take for granted that the correct interpretation of rights is the autonomy interpretation, according to which the function of rights is to protect our autonomy, rather than the dignity interpretation that I have proposed. They then support their claim, that possessive individualism belongs to the DNA of rights-talk, by telling one or another of two narratives concerning the origin of the idea of rights—or more precisely, concerning the origin of the idea of *natural* rights.

The more prominent of these two narratives was apparently originated by Leo Strauss in his 1953 publication *Natural Right and*

History.[1] According to Strauss, thinkers in the West traditionally thought in terms of objective right, not in terms of subjective rights. That is to say, they thought in terms of an objective order specifying the right thing to do in various situations; they did not think in terms of rights that individuals have or possess. The change, so Strauss claimed, occurred in Hobbes and Locke as part of their attempt to work out an individualistic, purely secular account of political authority. Strauss held that this change, from objective right to subjective rights, should be seen as a central component in the passage to modernity.

The alternative, less prominent, narrative was first told by the French legal historian Michel Villey in a number of publications in the 1950s. Villey was a neo-Thomist who, like most neo-Thomists, viewed Thomas Aquinas as the apogee of Western philosophy and regarded everything after Thomas as either a decline from the heights or an attempt to regain them. Villey argued that when it came to the idea of natural rights, the fall from grace came with the nominalist philosopher William of Ockham in the early 1300s. In the course of defending his fellow Franciscans against attacks from the papacy, Ockham introduced the idea of natural rights, so said Villey. Strauss saw the idea of natural subjective rights as born of individualist political philosophy; Villey saw the idea as born of philosophical nominalism. And both Strauss and Villey assumed that the idea cannot be freed from the philosophical framework that gave it birth.[2]

We now know that both of these narratives are false. In his groundbreaking book *The Idea of Natural Rights: Studies on Natural Rights, Natural Law and Church Law 1150–1625*,[3] Brian Tierney shows that in the latter part of the 1100s, thus more than a century before Ockham, canon lawyers were employing the concept of natural rights in their comments on the legal texts (assembled by the Italian professor

1. Leo Strauss, *Natural Right and History* (Chicago: University of Chicago Press, 1953).

2. In the second chapter of my *Justice: Rights and Wrongs* (Princeton: Princeton University Press, 2008), I relate both of these narratives in considerable detail.

3. Brian Tierney, *The Idea of Natural Rights: Studies on Natural Rights, Natural Law and Church Law 1150–1625* (Atlanta: Scholars Press, 1997).

Gratian around 1140) that came to be called *Decretum Gratiani*, and in their discussion of ecclesiastical legal issues of the day. Charles J. Reid Jr., a student of Tierney, fleshes out the story in his *Power over the Body, Equality in the Family: Rights and Domestic Relations in Medieval Canon Law*.[4] John Witte, in his book *The Reformation of Rights*,[5] shows that the idea of natural rights was in common use among writers in various branches of the early Protestant Reformation, especially the Reformed (Calvinist) branch. And Richard Tuck, in *Natural Rights Theories: Their Origin and Development*,[6] tells the story of appeals to natural rights in the late Middle Ages and early Renaissance. We can assume that the canon lawyers of the twelfth century were not possessive individualists in their mentality, and that neither were their successors, the Spanish theologians of the Renaissance, and the Reformation theologians of the sixteenth and seventeenth centuries.

Only if one has forgotten the role of the idea of natural rights in the thought of the early Calvinist theologians would the Strauss narrative seem plausible; and only if one has forgotten the work of the canon lawyers of the twelfth century would the Villey narrative seem plausible. Cultural amnesia was required for the Strauss and Villey narratives to become popular.

The idea of natural rights originated in the seedbed of medieval Christendom. It did not originate in the Enlightenment with Hobbes and Locke; Hobbes and Locke employed what they had been bequeathed. The idea does not carry possessive individualism in its DNA.

It's an abuse of rights-talk to employ it in the service of possessive individualism. The other comes into my presence as a creature of worth; I likewise come into her presence as a creature of worth. On account of her worth, she has legitimate claims on me as to how

4. Charles J. Reid Jr., *Power over the Body, Equality in the Family: Rights and Domestic Relations in Medieval Canon Law* (Grand Rapids: Eerdmans, 2004).

5. John Witte, *The Reformation of Rights* (Cambridge: Cambridge University Press, 2007).

6. Richard Tuck, *Natural Rights Theories: Their Origin and Development* (Cambridge: Cambridge University Press, 1979).

I treat her; on account of my worth, I have legitimate claims on her as to how she treats me. If she is not treated by me as she has a right to be treated, she has been wronged by me; if I am not treated by her as I have a right to be treated, I have been wronged by her. The language of rights is for bringing this reality to speech.

PART 3

JUSTICE IN SCRIPTURE

❖11❖

Natural Rights
in Three Church Fathers

From Tierney's groundbreaking work we learn that it was not the secular political philosophers of the Enlightenment but the canon lawyers of the twelfth century who were the first to employ the concept of natural rights in a sustained and systematic way. That suggests the following question: Though natural rights were not systematically conceptualized before the twelfth century, may it nonetheless be the case that their existence was taken for granted earlier? We all take many things for granted that we don't explicitly conceptualize.

Writing on the topic of poverty, Ambrose of Milan, one of the Latin church fathers (340–397), said, "Not from your own do you bestow upon the poor man, but you make return from what is his."[1] Speaking at somewhat greater length on the same topic, one of the Greek fathers, Basil the Great of Caesarea (330–379), said this:

---

1. I am quoting from the translation in Charles Avila, *Ownership: Early Christian Teaching* (Maryknoll, NY: Orbis Books, 1983), 50.

Will not one be called a thief who steals the garment of one already clothed, and is one deserving of any other title who will not clothe the naked if he is able to do so? That bread which you keep, belongs to the hungry; that coat which you preserve in your wardrobe, to the naked; those shoes which are rotting in your possession, to the shoeless; that gold which you have hidden in the ground, to the needy. Wherefore, as often as you were able to help others, and refused, so often did you do them wrong.[2]

And speaking on the same topic at yet greater length, here is what John Chrysostom (347–407), the great preacher of Antioch and Constantinople, said in the second of his series of sermons on the parable of Lazarus and the rich man:

This also is theft, not to share one's possessions. Perhaps this statement seems surprising to you, but do not be surprised. I shall bring you testimony from the divine Scriptures, saying that not only the theft of others' goods but also the failure to share one's own goods with others is theft and swindle and defraudation. . . . The Scripture says, "Deprive not the poor of his living." To deprive is to take what belongs to another; for it is called deprivation when we take and keep what belongs to others. . . .

The rich man is a kind of steward of the money which is owed for distribution to the poor. He is directed to distribute it to his fellow servants who are in want. So if he spends more on himself than his need requires, he will pay the harshest penalty hereafter. For his own goods are not his own, but belong to his fellow servants.

The poor man has one plea, his want and his standing in need: do not require anything else from him; but even if he is the most wicked of all men and is at a loss for his necessary sustenance, let us free him from hunger. . . . The almsgiver is a harbor for those in necessity: a harbor receives all who have encountered shipwreck and frees them from danger; whether they are bad or good or whatever they are who are in danger, it escorts them into its own shelter. So you likewise, when you see on earth the man who has encountered the shipwreck of

2. Ibid., 66.

poverty, do not judge him, do not seek an account of his life, but free him from his misfortune. . . .

Need alone is the poor man's worthiness; if anyone at all ever comes to us with this recommendation, let us not meddle any further. We do not provide for the manners but for the man. We show mercy on him not because of his virtue but because of his misfortune, in order that we ourselves may receive from the Master His great mercy. . . .

I beg you, remember this without fail, that not to share our own wealth with the poor is theft from the poor and deprivation of their means of life; we do not possess our own wealth but theirs.[3]

This is striking language. No doubt Ambrose, Basil, and John believed that some of the poor were impoverished because they were guilty of being lazy. But they don't say that—not in these passages; they do not lay guilt on the poor. Nor do they try to evoke pity in the rich so that they will be moved to contribute generously to the local benevolence fund. They do not praise the virtue of charity. Clearly they believed that the rich would be failing in their obligations if they refused to share with the poor, but that too is not what they emphasize.

Rather than pointing to the moral condition of the stingy rich, Ambrose, Basil, and John give voice to the moral condition of the unaided poor. They say that the extra clothes in the closet of the well-to-do person *belong to* the poor person who lacks clothes, that the extra food in the cupboard of the well-to-do person *belongs to* the poor person who has little. They declare, in other words, that the poor person has a *right* to those clothes and a *right* to that food. If something belongs to you, then you have a right to it, a legitimate claim. Failure to share one's possessions is theft, swindle, fraud, says John. Basil adds that the well-to-do person who refuses to aid the poor person *wrongs* that person. It is, of course, a *natural* right that Ambrose, Basil, and John have in mind, not a right bestowed by the local laws; they do not appeal to the local laws.

John adds that the right of the poor to means of sustenance does not depend on their good behavior. Those who have encountered

3. St. John Chrysostom, *On Wealth and Poverty*, trans. Catherine P. Roth (Crestwood, NY: St. Vladimir's Seminary Press, 1984), 49–55.

the shipwreck of poverty are not required to give an account of their lives. Rather than judging them, we must free them from their misfortune. We come to their aid because of their plight, not because of their virtue.

Where did this striking way of thinking about the moral significance of poverty come from? Did Ambrose, Basil, John, and others among the church fathers invent it? Alternatively, did they get it from their pagan Greek and Roman inheritance?

Neither. As John indicates, it came from the Bible. The archaeology of rights leads us ineluctably from the political thinkers of the Enlightenment to the early Calvinist theologians, from the early Calvinist theologians to the Spanish theologians of the pre-Reformation, from the Spanish theologians of the pre-Reformation to the canon lawyers of the twelfth century, from the canon lawyers of the twelfth century to the church fathers, and from the church fathers to Christian Scripture.

But I am getting ahead of myself. This archaeology of natural rights came rather late in my thinking about rights; Tierney's book was not published until 1997, Witte's not until 2007. It was not this archaeology that led me to justice in the Hebrew and Christian Scriptures but those faces and voices that I encountered.

Justice in the Old Testament

I was reared in the Christian church. My particular tradition, an American transplant of the Dutch Reformed tradition, made much of Scripture, both Old Testament and New. We read a great deal of Scripture, and we sang the Psalms.

Christian Scripture speaks often and emphatically about justice. I would have heard and read many of the passages about justice; in singing the Psalms I would have sung about justice. But it all passed me by. Nobody called it to my attention; nothing in my situation made it jump out. My church had a benevolence fund; it did not have a social justice committee.

My parents were poor, very poor. But it never occurred to me to think that our poverty was the result of injustice somewhere along the line. As it turned out, it was. Fifty years after the fact I learned that my father had been fired from his position in the village grocery store on the charge of embezzlement. Anyone who knew my father would have found the charge preposterous. Some years after he was fired it came to light that the embezzler was the son of the owner. At the time, I knew nothing of all this.

Upon returning from Potchefstroom, with the cry for justice ringing in my ears, I continued to do what I had always done: I listened to Scripture read liturgically, I read it for myself, I sang the Psalms. But my listening and reading and singing were different now. The references to justice that had passed me by now jumped out. My encounter with the people of color in South Africa and with the Palestinians had opened my eyes and focused my attention.

Though Christian Scripture speaks often about justice, it neither gives a definition nor offers a theory of justice. It assumes that we know well enough what justice is. What it does do, over and over, is enjoin its readers to act justly and to right injustice. It enjoins them to do so out of love for justice. It sets those imperatives within a theological context that explains why we should love justice, why we should right injustice, and how we should understand what we are doing when we act justly and right injustice. And it establishes priorities for doing justice and for seeking to right injustice.

"Justice, and only justice, you shall follow," says Moses in the divine law code that he delivered as part of his farewell address to the people of Israel, "that you may live and inherit the land which the LORD your God gives you" (Deut. 16:20). The command to do justice and to right injustice is intensified in the Prophets, who often contrast acting justly with going through the motions of piety. In a well-known passage from the prophet Amos, God says,

> I hate, I despise your feasts,
>> and I take no delight in your solemn assemblies.
> Even though you offer me your burnt offerings and cereal
>> offerings,
>> I will not accept them,
> and the peace offerings of your fatted beasts
>> I will not look upon.
> Take away from me the noise of your songs;
>> to the melody of your harps I will not listen.
> But let justice roll down like waters,
>> and righteousness like an ever-flowing stream. (5:21–24)

The same command to act justly occurs in an equally well-known passage from Micah 6 (quoted in the NRSV). The passage opens with intense poignancy as God expresses pained lament to Israel—not human beings lamenting to God but God lamenting to human beings.

> O my people, what have I done to you?
>> In what have I wearied you? Answer me!
> For I brought you up from the land of Egypt,
>> and redeemed you from the house of slavery. (vv. 3–4)

The prophet imagines someone who, stung by this divine lament, asks what would please God and ease God's sorrow.

> With what shall I come before the LORD,
>> and bow myself before God on high?
> Shall I come before him with burnt offerings,
>> with calves a year old? (v. 6)

The imagined speaker resorts to hyperbole.

> Will the LORD be pleased with thousands of rams,
>> with ten thousands of rivers of oil? (v. 7)

The prophet brushes the speaker's questions aside.

> He has told you, O mortal, what is good;
>> and what does the LORD require of you
> but to do justice, and to love kindness,
>> and to walk humbly with your God? (v. 8)

The theological background for the injunction to do justice is that God loves justice and hates injustice. To read Isaiah 61 is to hear God saying, "I the LORD love justice" (61:8). To join Israel and the church in taking on one's own lips the words of Psalm 37 is to find oneself saying that "the LORD loves justice" (v. 28). These are but two examples from many. It is God's love of justice that lies behind

God's injunction to us to do justice and to right injustice. We are to imitate God.

A different aspect of the theological background to Scripture's injunction to do justice and right injustice comes to light in another passage from the law code that Moses delivered as part of his farewell address.

> You shall not pervert the justice due to the sojourner or to the fatherless, or take a widow's garment in pledge; but you shall remember that you were a slave in Egypt and the LORD your God redeemed you from there; therefore I command you to do this.
>
> When you reap your harvest in your field, and have forgotten a sheaf in the field, you shall not go back to get it; it shall be for the sojourner, the fatherless, and the widow; that the LORD your God may bless you in all the work of your hands. When you beat your olive trees, you shall not go over the boughs again; it shall be for the sojourner, the fatherless, and the widow. When you gather the grapes of your vineyard, you shall not glean it afterward; it shall be for the sojourner, the fatherless, and the widow. You shall remember that you were a slave in the land of Egypt; therefore I command you to do this. (Deut. 24:17–22)

This is strange. The members of Israel are to treat justly the widows, the fatherless, and the sojourners in their midst so as to remember that they, as a people, were themselves once slaves in Egypt and that God redeemed them from their slavery. What's the connection between treating widows, sojourners, and the fatherless justly, and remembering that God delivered Israel from slavery?

Of course, *while* they are practicing justice, the Israelites can recall that they were delivered; they can do those two things simultaneously. But God is commanding them to do justice *because* they are to remember that they were delivered—or perhaps *so that* they remember, or *as a way* of remembering. What sense does that make? How can one treat someone justly *because* one remembers the deliverance of one's people? How can one treat someone justly *so that* one remembers, or *as a way* of remembering?

The clue to the answer is that the reference to remembering is not a reference to the private interior act of keeping in mind or recalling but to the public social act of *doing something as a memorial*. In many places in the Old Testament God is reported as instructing Israel to do or make something as a memorial; Israel's social life is to be filled with memorial acts and memorial objects. The best known of these Old Testament memorials is the Passover; we read in Exodus that the Passover "shall be for you a memorial day" (12:14).

What is it to do or make something as a memorial? Some biblical scholars claim that this idea of doing or making something as a memorial, or as a remembrance, was peculiar to the ancient Israelites, or perhaps to the ancient Semitic people generally. It is said that whereas we modern people think of remembering as something interior and private, the ancient Israelites or Semites thought of remembering as external and social.

The claim has to be rejected. You and I, modern people, do and make things as memorials; our lives are filled with memorial actions and memorial objects. We issue coins as memorials, we hold conferences as memorials, we name cities as memorials. The Vietnam Veterans Memorial in Washington, DC, is a memorial—what else could it be? Americans celebrate every Fourth of July as a memorial or commemoration of the signing of the Declaration of Independence.

Why do we do this? Why do we do and make things as memorials? We do this in order to honor important persons and events from our past and to keep their memory alive. The Vietnam Veterans Memorial honors those Americans who gave their lives in the Vietnam War and keeps alive their memory; naming our national capital "Washington" honors George Washington and keeps alive his memory. We human beings are forgetful; we forget even those persons and events from our past that we want to honor. Doing or making something as a memorial is a way of honoring that simultaneously compensates for our forgetfulness.

But why were the Israelites *to do justice* to widows, sojourners, and the fatherless as a memorial of their deliverance by God from enslavement in Egypt? Why *do justice* as a memorial? Why not something else? And why do justice *to these people*?

There were in fact other things that Israel did as a memorial of its deliverance from Egypt. It celebrated the Passover meal annually as a memorial of its deliverance; it rested on the seventh day of the week as a memorial of its deliverance.

It's easy to see why a day of rest would be regarded as an appropriate thing to do as a memorial of deliverance from slave labor. But once again, why would treating justly the widows, the fatherless, and the sojourners be regarded as appropriate?

The answer, I think, is the following. The picture one gets from the Old Testament as a whole is that the well-being of widows, sojourners, and the fatherless was seriously endangered in ancient Israel. They were the vulnerable ones. Treating them justly delivered them from danger. That's why treating them justly was appropriate as a memorial of Israel's deliverance from enslavement in Egypt.

Add that if this was indeed what made it appropriate to treat justly these groups as a memorial of God's deliverance of Israel from Egypt, then, in treating them justly, Israel was imitating God. It was doing both things at once: doing justice to the vulnerable as a memorial of its deliverance from Egypt, and imitating God.

I mentioned earlier that Scripture gives neither a definition nor a theory of justice; instead it enjoins us to seek justice, it places this injunction within a theological context that tells us why we should seek justice and how we should understand what we are doing when we do seek justice, and it establishes priorities for doing justice and for seeking to right injustice. We have taken note of the major components of the theological context. Let me now say something about priorities. We can begin with the same passage from Deuteronomy that I have been commenting on.

Four times within the space of six brief verses the passage connects doing justice with the fate of the widow, the fatherless, and the sojourner. The passage is typical, in this respect, of the Old Testament in general. Over and over the doing of justice and the righting of injustice are connected to the fate of widows, orphans, and resident aliens—to which is often added the poor. Here is Isaiah speaking:

> Seek justice,
>   rescue the oppressed,
> defend the orphan,
>   plead for the widow. (1:17 NRSV)

A few chapters later we read:

> Woe to those who decree iniquitous decrees,
>   and the writers who keep writing oppression,
> to turn aside the needy from justice
>   and to rob the poor of my people of their right,
> that widows may be their spoil,
>   and that they may make the fatherless their prey! (Isa.
>   10:1–2)

From the hundreds of additional passages that could be cited to make the point, let me add just one more, this from the Psalms:

> Give justice to the weak and the orphan;
>   maintain the right of the lowly and the destitute.
> Rescue the weak and the needy;
>   deliver them from the hand of the wicked. (Ps. 82:3–4
>   NRSV)

Plato's *Republic* is all about justice. But nowhere in the *Republic* is justice connected to the fate of the widow, the orphan, the resident alien, and the poor. That's partly because Plato's main project in the *Republic* is to develop a version of "ideal theory," as Rawls calls it. Along the way, however, Plato highlights various ways in which the ideal republic is liable to break down. The breakdowns he highlights all consist of people doing things other than what they are best fitted to do; they do not consist of widows, orphans, aliens, and the impoverished living an endangered existence.

What's true of Plato's discussion of justice is true of most literature of the West about justice. The connection that the Old Testament writers draw between justice, on the one hand, and the fate of widows, orphans, resident aliens, and the impoverished, on the other hand, is unusual, extraordinary, striking—so striking that we are bound to ask, what does it mean? What is its significance?

The Old Testament writers were by no means oblivious to the importance of a well-functioning system of judicial and criminal justice. The line that I quoted from Moses's farewell address, "Justice, and only justice, you shall follow," comes at the end of a passage in which Moses instructs Israel to institute a judicial system that judges justly. The judges are not to show partiality; they are not to take bribes; they are not to "pervert justice." But the widows, the orphans, the resident aliens, and the impoverished were not, in general, wrongdoers; the justice due them was not criminal justice but primary justice and the righting of primary injustice. When the Old Testament writers say that God *loves* justice, they do not mean that God loves seeing people punished. So once again: Why the repetitive mention of the widows, the orphans, the aliens, and the impoverished when primary justice and injustice are in view?

The South American liberation theologians of a few decades back argued that what is coming to the surface here is God's "preferential option for the poor," as they called it. This suggestion infuriated a good many well-to-do North American Christians. "What do you mean, God's preferential option for the poor? Doesn't God love everybody equally, rich and poor alike? One doesn't have to be poor to be loved by God. And besides, aren't we all poor in God's sight?"

God does indeed love one and all; one does not have to be poor to be loved by God. Yet there is no getting around the fact that God's declaration that he loves justice, and God's instruction to us to do justice and to right injustice, is over and over connected in Scripture with the fate of the widows, the orphans, the aliens, and the impoverished. Why is that? Why the preferential option for the poor—or more generally, for the widows, the orphans, and the resident aliens along with the poor? Why the preferential option for the vulnerable? For that's what these four groups were—the vulnerable, *the quartet of the vulnerable.*

Let me make some suggestions. First, the reference of the biblical writers to justice is never in the context of an abstract discourse on the nature of justice but always in the context of the injunction to do justice and to right injustice; and that injunction is never addressed to the denizens of some imagined ideal society but to the inhabitants of an actual fallen society. Second, when we seek to do justice and to right injustice in our actual fallen societies, we have to set priorities. Nobody can do justice to everybody; nobody can right all injustice. Third, powerful and wealthy people do on occasion get mugged, burglarized, and so forth. They too are the victims of injustice—the victims of *episodes* of injustice. But compare that to the situation of the widows, the orphans, the aliens, and the impoverished in old Israel. Their *daily condition* was unjust, or highly vulnerable to being unjust. They too would have suffered *episodes* of injustice: muggings, for example. But their daily condition was *systemically* unjust, or highly vulnerable to being *systemically* unjust.

If one is seeking to do justice and to right injustice, one will not ignore episodic injustices, but one will give priority to systemic injustice. One will give priority to the fate of those whose daily condition is unjust, or especially vulnerable to being unjust. That's why there was a preferential option for the quartet of the vulnerable.

A final point. In one of the passages that I quoted from Isaiah, the prophet describes the quartet of the vulnerable as "oppressed"; in one of the passages that I quoted from the Psalms, the songwriter describes them as in "the hand of the wicked." In a good many other passages they are described as *downtrodden.*

Isaiah and the psalmist do not describe them as "unfortunates," a term one hears in many quarters nowadays. To describe them as "unfortunates" is to suggest that nobody is responsible for their condition; nobody is guilty. It may be that we would wrong them if we walked by and did nothing to alleviate their plight; alleviating their plight would then be a matter of justice, not of optional charity. But since their plight is not the consequence of injustice, treating them justly does not include seeking to right injustice.

By contrast, to describe them as *downtrodden* is to imply that their condition is the consequence of injustice; and that, in turn, implies that someone is responsible for their condition. To describe them as downtrodden is to imply moral critique. Moral critique typically arouses defensiveness and anger, sometimes threats, sometimes even assassinations. I will have more to say about that later.

❖ 13 ❖

On the Claim
That Justice Is Supplanted
in the New Testament

I have said nothing about the role of justice in the New Testament; I have confined myself to speaking about its role in the Old Testament. I have done so deliberately, in order to be able to confront head-on the popular view that, in the New Testament, the injunction to do justice and to seek to right injustice has been abrogated and supplanted.

One finds two rather different lines of thought employed to support this conclusion. One line of thought holds that though it's true that God continues to love justice and to have a special concern for the vulnerable, it is not your and my business to seek to reform those social structures that oppress people, nor is it your and my business to press government to bring wrongdoers to justice. Change in oppressive and corrupt social structures can happen only if those who inhabit these structures have a change of heart. Absent changed hearts, the struggle for reform is futile. The New Testament instructs us to seek changed hearts. In heaven there will be justice; all those who are faithful will be vindicated. But for that day we do not work; we wait. God and God alone will bring it about. The fundamental posture of the Christian in this world is waiting—waiting in patience and hope to be released from this present evil world and to enter heaven.

This line of thought is correct in holding that expectant waiting is a fundamental component of New Testament spirituality. As Paul puts it in his Letter to the Romans,

> For the creation waits with eager longing for the revealing of the children of God; for . . . the creation itself will be set free from its bondage to decay and will obtain the freedom of the glory of the children of God. We know that the whole creation has been groaning in labor pains until now; and not only the creation, but we ourselves, who have the first fruits of the Spirit, groan inwardly while we wait for adoption, the redemption of our bodies. For in hope we were saved. . . . But if we hope for what we do not see, we wait for it with patience. (Rom. 8:19–25 NRSV)

But the fact that expectant waiting for the new creation is a fundamental component of New Testament spirituality does not establish the correctness of this first line of thought. The question to consider is the *form* that our waiting is to take. Are we to resign ourselves to the injustice of this world while patiently waiting for the coming of the new creation to sweep it all away, or are we to struggle for its alleviation while patiently waiting for the coming of the new creation to bring our efforts to fruition? Are we to await the fulfillment of our social endeavors as well as the fulfillment of our social hopes, or are we to await only the fulfillment of our social hopes?

On a recent trip to Honduras, about which I will say more later, I learned that a great many evangelical Christians in that country reason as follows: they equate justice with the state bringing wrongdoers to judgment and punishing them, they equate punishment with retribution, and then they quote Paul in Romans: "Vengeance is mine, I will repay, says the Lord" (Rom. 12:19; quoting Deut. 32:35). The conclusion drawn is that it is not our business to seek justice.

A second line of thought employed to support the claim that, in the New Testament, the injunction to do justice and to seek to right injustice has been abrogated, is found less in popular piety and more in a movement within twentieth-century Protestant ethics and theology. The Greek word that the New Testament writers used to report Jesus's injunction to love God above all and one's neighbor as oneself is *agapē*. The central claim of the movement I have in mind is that what Jesus meant by *agapē* was gratuitous self-sacrificing benevolence that pays no attention to what justice requires. The classic text of the movement is the book published in the early 1930s by the Swedish Lutheran bishop Anders Nygren, *Agape and Eros*.[1] In *Agape and Eros* Nygren never mentions the nineteenth-century Danish Lutheran philosopher Søren Kierkegaard, but it's hard to believe that Nygren's understanding of *agapē* in the New Testament was not influenced by Kierkegaard's *Works of Love*.

Of the two, Nygren and Kierkegaard, Kierkegaard was undoubtedly the more profound. But not only did Nygren have more influence among theologians, he also devoted a good deal more attention to the relation between love and justice than Kierkegaard did. His claim is that agapic love supplants justice in the New Testament. Let's look at how he developed this idea.

Nygren saw three great motifs, as he called them, locked in a struggle for dominance in Western thought. One motif is that of *eros*, eros being love as attraction. The motif of eros is dominant in the Platonic tradition; it's the topic of Plato's discussion in his *Symposium*. (Nygren

---

1. In *Justice in Love* (Grand Rapids: Eerdmans, 2011), I refer to the movement I have in mind as "modern-day agapism." That may have been a mistake, since at least one reviewer assumes I had in mind all twentieth-century Christian ethicists for whom *agapē* was a central category in their thought; he then excoriates me for falsely claiming that all of these twentieth-century ethicists were explicit or implicit "Nygrenists" in their understanding of New Testament *agapē*. This interpretation should have been forestalled by the following words that open the book's chapter on modern-day agapism: "In the twentieth century there emerged among Christian (especially Protestant) ethicists and theologians, a highly articulate and provocative version of agapism, with Søren Kierkegaard as its great nineteenth-century forebear. . . . At the core of the movement was a distinctive and sharply delineated interpretation of what Jesus meant by 'love'" (ibid., 21).

argued that eros is a form of self-love. This seems to me highly implausible. When I say that I love Beethoven's late string quartets, it is
love as attraction that I have in mind; but it's the quartets that I love,
not myself.) A second motif is that of *nomos*, law. Nygren associated
nomos with justice, and he held that the motif of nomos is dominant
in the Old Testament. The third motif is *agapē*, understood as self-
sacrificial benevolence or generosity that pays no attention to what
justice requires. The motif of agape, so Nygren argued, is dominant
in the New Testament; it is the love that Jesus attributes to God and
that he enjoins on us for the neighbor.

Nygren unhesitatingly affirmed the implication of this scheme, that
the Old Testament motif of justice has been supplanted in the New
Testament by the motif of agapic love. The Old Testament God is a
god of justice; the New Testament God is a god of love. Jesus, says
Nygren, "enters into fellowship with those who are not worthy of it."
His doing so is directed "against every attempt to regulate fellowship
with God by the principle of justice."[2] "That Jesus should take lost
sinners to Himself was bound to appear, not only to the Pharisees,
but to anyone brought up and rooted in Jewish legal righteousness,
as a violation of the order established by God Himself and guaran-
teed by His justice."[3] For them it was "a violation not only of the
human, but above all of the Divine, order of justice, and therefore
of God's majesty."[4]

In short, the agapic love displayed and enjoined by Jesus does not
incorporate or supplement justice; it supersedes it. "'Motivated' justice
must give place . . . to 'unmotivated' love."[5] We are not to love the
neighbor agapically *in addition to* treating her as justice requires; we
are to love her agapically *instead of* treating her as justice requires.

Why did Nygren see love as supplanting justice in the New Testament? Why not love *and* justice? Nygren's answer to this question

2. Anders Nygren, *Agape and Eros*, trans. Philip S. Watson (London: SPCK, 1953),
86.
3. Ibid., 83.
4. Ibid., 70.
5. Ibid., 74.

was admirably clear. He held that the paradigmatic New Testament example of love, the example that should shape all our thinking about love, both God's love of us and our love of neighbor, is God's loving forgiveness of the sinner. God's forgiveness is not a case of doing what justice requires; the wrongdoer cannot claim that justice requires that God forgive him.

Our love of the neighbor is to imitate God's forgiveness. Out of gratuitous generosity we are to seek to advance her well-being, paying no attention to what justice requires. The love that Jesus and the New Testament writers had in mind expels any note of doing what justice requires. New Testament love is blind to what justice requires. It is an utterly gratuitous, self-sacrificing concern for the well-being of the other.

Nygren took this line of thought a step further. In its blindness to what justice requires, agapic love may perpetrate injustice. Nygren regarded this as the point of Jesus's parable of the laborers in the vineyard (Matt. 20:1–16). The landlord, on Nygren's interpretation, acknowledges that when he paid the latecomers the same amount as those who worked all day in the heat, he was being unfair and unjust to the early workers. But the landowner dismisses the grumbling of the early workers with the remark that he has a right to be generous as he wishes. Nygren drew the lesson that we must expect that agapic love—self-giving generosity that pays no attention to what justice requires—will sometimes wreak injustice. No matter. The follower of Jesus is called to remain faithful to love even at the cost of wreaking injustice.

After Nygren, the figure in the modern-day agapist movement who thought most deeply about the relation of New Testament love to justice was the American theologian Reinhold Niebuhr. Niebuhr joined Nygren in interpreting New Testament love as gratuitous self-giving generosity that pays no attention to what justice requires, and he agreed with Nygren that such love might perpetrate injustice. But Niebuhr thought that Nygren's response to the possibility of conflict between love and justice was socially and politically naive.

Stick with love, said Nygren. Niebuhr thought that as a social and political policy, this would be a calamity. Try responding to Hitler with agapic love! A major part of Niebuhr's lifelong opposition to American liberal Christianity was his opposition to what he saw as its naive assumption that if Christians would just love their neighbors more, people would respond in kind, and love would eventually rule the world. In this present age, said Niebuhr, we must expect that love will often not evoke love but instead perpetrate or abet injustice and get run over. The life of Jesus ended on the cross.

So what to do? Niebuhr thought that it was deeply irresponsible to be content with perpetrating or abetting injustice. Yet as a Christian theologian and ethicist he could not give up on love. His solution was to argue that justice is for this present fallen world of conflicting interests, whereas agapic love is for the eschaton of "frictionless harmony," as he called it. To this he added the qualification that here and now, in small-scale situations where conflict is absent and agapic love can be practiced without aiding and abetting injustice, we should love the neighbor.

❖14❖

Justice in the New Testament

Nygren's line of thought is untenable—and Niebuhr's as well, for somewhat different reasons. Let me focus on Nygren. Nygren's line of thought is systematically incoherent. We are always to think of love on the model of God's forgiveness of the sinner, says Nygren; accordingly, since forgiveness is not required by justice, we should pay no attention to what justice requires. But reflect for a moment on the nature of forgiveness. One cannot just spread forgiveness hither and yon. I can forgive someone for what he did to me only if he wronged me, only *for* the wrong he did to me, and only if I recognize that he wronged me. But to wrong someone is to treat that person unjustly; it is to deprive him of something to which he has a right. So forgiveness cannot be blind to justice and injustice. Forgiveness presupposes attentiveness to injustice. Forgiveness does indeed go beyond what justice requires; the wrongdoer does not have a right to be forgiven. But forgiveness is a response to injustice and to the recognition of injustice. To put justice and injustice out of mind is to put forgiveness out of mind.

The reply may be forthcoming that though it's true that forgiveness cannot be inattentive to injustice—Nygren was mistaken about that—nonetheless it remains the case that forgiveness is not *motivated* by what justice requires. True. But let us now take note of another and deeper incoherence in Nygren's claim that it is acceptable to perpetrate injustice out of agapic love.

If, in loving someone agapically, I treat him unjustly, then I violate his right not to be so treated; I wrong him. Now recall the Principle of Correlatives that I discussed earlier; the principle tells us that if someone has a right to my not treating him a certain way, then I have a correlative obligation toward him not to treat him that way. And recall the point I also made, that if I have an obligation not to treat him that way, then it is morally impermissible for me to treat him that way. Nygren's position implies that out of love, one is sometimes permitted to do what one ought not to do—namely, wrong someone. But that is incoherent. If I ought not to do it, then I am not *morally permitted* to do it.

More important for our purposes in this essay than either of these points of theoretical incoherence is the fact that Nygren's line of thought is exegetically untenable. For one thing, Nygren has misinterpreted the parable of the laborers in the vineyard—this being one of his main textual bases for saying that New Testament love may wreak injustice and that, when it does, the Christian must remain faithful to love and say good-bye to justice. The landowner in the parable does not say to the grumbling early workers what Nygren interprets him as saying—namely, "It's true that I have treated you unjustly, but don't I have a right to dispense my generosity as I wish?" Let me quote what the landowner does in fact say: "Friend, I am doing you no wrong; did you not agree with me for the usual daily wage? . . . I choose to give to this last the same as I give to you. Am I not allowed to do what I choose with what belongs to me?" (Matt. 20:13–15 NRSV). The Greek word translated here as "wrong" is *adikos*. "I am not treating you unjustly," says the landowner to the complainers. Rather than agreeing with them that he has treated them unjustly, but then insisting that this is an acceptable consequence of his generosity, the landowner insists that he has not treated them unjustly.

And now more generally. No careful reader of the New Testament could conclude that justice has been supplanted in the New Testament; justice runs like a scarlet thread throughout the New Testament. Begin with the fact that several of the identifications and self-identifications of Jesus in the Gospels depend essentially on justice.[1]

Jesus was extremely baffling and unsettling to those around him. Hence he repeatedly says who he is, and hence the Gospel writers tell us, in their own voice, who he is. The message of some of the most prominent of these identifications and self-identifications is that Jesus was anointed by God to inaugurate the day when justice shall reign.

In the fourth chapter of his Gospel, Luke tells the story of what happened when Jesus attended synagogue one Sabbath in his home village of Nazareth. He stood up to read, Luke says, and was handed the book of the prophet Isaiah. Jesus opened the book and found the place where it was written:

> The Spirit of the Lord is upon me,
>   because he has anointed me
> to bring good news to the poor.
> He has sent me to proclaim release to the captives
>   and recovery of sight to the blind,
> to let the oppressed go free,
> to proclaim the year of the Lord's favor. (Luke 4:18–19
>   NRSV)

Upon finishing his reading, Jesus closed the book, handed it back to the attendant, and sat down. The congregants all looked at him, expecting him to offer some commentary. He then said, "Today this scripture has been fulfilled in your hearing" (v. 21), thereby identifying himself as the Lord's anointed one of whom Isaiah spoke. Luke tells us that the congregants not only responded with approval but were amazed that Joseph's son would say such things. But when Jesus went on to suggest, using stories from the Old Testament about the

---

1. I develop more fully the points made in the following paragraphs in chapter 5 of my *Justice: Rights and Wrongs* (Princeton: Princeton University Press, 2008).

prophets Elijah and Elisha, that God's favor was not restricted to Israel, they were "filled with rage" (v. 28 NRSV).

The same self-identification, albeit a bit more allusive, occurs a few chapters later. When John the Baptist was in prison, dumped there by Herod, he received reports about Jesus from some of his followers. These reports disturbed him. He had been led to believe that Jesus was the Messiah and that he, John, was the Messiah's forerunner. But Jesus was not doing what John expected the Messiah to do. So John sent two of his disciples to Jesus with the question, "Are you the one who is to come, or are we to wait for another?" (7:19 NRSV). They put their question to Jesus after Jesus had "cured many people of diseases, plagues, and evil spirits, and had given sight to many who were blind" (v. 21 NRSV). The answer Jesus gave John's disciples resembles his earlier self-identification in the synagogue: "Go and tell John what you have seen and heard: the blind receive their sight, the lame walk, the lepers are cleansed, the deaf hear, the dead are raised, the poor have good news brought to them" (v. 22 NRSV). Jesus then declared as blessed "anyone who takes no offense" at him (v. 23 NRSV).

In Matthew's Gospel we find a closely similar identification, this time in the Gospel writer's own voice. In Matthew's telling of the story of Jesus, Jesus has already been teaching and healing for some time when Matthew intrudes himself into the story and offers his own interpretation of the significance of the events he has been narrating. "This was to fulfill what had been spoken through the prophet Isaiah":

> Here is my servant, whom I have chosen,
>   my beloved, with whom my soul is well pleased.
> I will put my Spirit upon him,
>   and he will proclaim justice [*krisis*] to the Gentiles. . . .
> He will not break a bruised reed
>   or quench a smoldering wick
> until he brings justice [*krisis*] to victory.
>   And in his name the Gentiles will hope. (Matt. 12:17–18,
>   20–21 NRSV)

What are we to make of these identifications? Begin by noting that in his report of what transpired in the synagogue, Luke adapted the opening two verses of Isaiah 61. The opening and closing lines of what Luke reports Jesus as reading are exactly as they are in Isaiah. But Luke added a line ("recovery of sight to the blind"), dropped a line ("to bind up the brokenhearted"), and changed the line "release to the prisoners" so that it reads "to let the oppressed go free." The entire passage from Isaiah goes as follows:

> The Spirit of the Lord God is upon me,
>> because the Lord has anointed me;
> he has sent me to bring good news to the oppressed;
>> to bind up the brokenhearted,
> to proclaim liberty to the captives,
>> and release to the prisoners;
> to proclaim the year of the Lord's favor. (Isa. 61:1–2 NRSV)

This passage bears strong similarities to another passage from three chapters earlier in Isaiah. Like the passage from Micah quoted in chapter 12, this earlier passage in Isaiah is preceded by a rejection of the piety of those who wreak injustice: "Behold, in the day of your fast you seek your own pleasure, and oppress all your workers. . . . Fasting like yours this day will not make your voice to be heard on high" (58:3–4). The passage then goes as follows:

> Is not this the fast that I choose:
>> to loose the bonds of wickedness,
>> to undo the thongs of the yoke,
> to let the oppressed go free,
>> and to break every yoke?
> Is it not to share your bread with the hungry,
>> and bring the homeless poor into your house;
> when you see the naked, to cover him,
>> and not to hide yourself from your own flesh? (58:6–7)

Anyone schooled in Scripture, as Jesus and his listeners obviously were, would immediately have recognized bringing good news to the poor, proclaiming release to the captives, and letting the oppressed go free as standard Old Testament examples of doing justice. Jesus identifies himself, and is identified by the Gospel writers, as God's chosen one appointed to inaugurate God's reign of justice.

We have caught a glimpse of the role of justice in the New Testament. There is more to be seen, much more. But in order to discern that "more" we have to deal with an issue of English translation of the New Testament.

❖ 15 ❖

On English Translations of the New Testament

I have often asked myself (and others) why so many people find it plausible that justice has been supplanted in the New Testament. Nobody disputes that justice is prominent in the Old Testament. The Old Testament is an extraordinarily rich and diverse collection of writings. In one's preoccupation with other themes, one may overlook the theme of justice; that is understandable. But once the issue is raised, nobody disputes that justice is prominent in the Old Testament.

Why is the New Testament not interpreted in continuity with the Old Testament on this point? Why is it interpreted as breaking with the Old Testament? The writers of the Old Testament proclaim that God loves justice. Why is the God of the New Testament not also understood as loving justice? The God of the Old Testament enjoins us to do justice and to seek to right injustice. Why is the God of the New Testament not also understood as enjoining us to do justice and to seek to right injustice?

Nygren had a theological hermeneutic principle that shaped his thought: all love, both divine and human, is to be viewed through the lens of God's gracious forgiveness of the sinner. But if the application of this principle leads to the conclusion that love has supplanted justice in the New Testament, why not, in the face of all the evidence to the contrary, back up and conclude that there's something mistaken in viewing all love through that lens? Why not rethink one's understanding of love?

The Latin word for justice was *justitia*. The Romance languages—Italian, Spanish, Portuguese, French, Romanian—are direct descendants of Latin. In translations of the New Testament into one or another of those languages there are a good many occurrences of their Latin-based word for justice—in Spanish, *justicia*. By contrast, most English translations of the New Testament seldom use the words *justice*, *just*, *unjust*, and so forth. That contributes to making Nygren's thesis seem plausible to those who read the New Testament in English. The New Testament they read seldom speaks about justice.

In the original Greek of the New Testament, one often comes across the adjective *dikaios*, the noun *dikaiosynē*, the verb *dikaioō*, and so forth—*dik*-stem words. I studied classical Greek before I read the New Testament in Greek. One of the books we read when studying classical Greek was Plato's *Republic*. *Dik*-stem words are common in the *Republic*. We were taught to translate them, pretty much automatically, as "justice," "just," "justly," and so forth. The topic of the *Republic* is justice.

I well remember my surprise when first I read the New Testament in Greek, found lots of occurrences there of *dik*-stem words—somewhere between three and four hundred—but discovered that, in most English translations of the New Testament, the adjective is almost always translated as "righteous" rather than "just," the noun as "righteousness" rather than "justice," and so forth. Not always. At the dinner party hosted by a Pharisee that Luke reports Jesus as attending one Sabbath, Jesus says to the host, "When you give a feast, invite the poor, the maimed, the lame, the blind, and you will be blessed, because they cannot repay you. You will be repaid at the resurrection of the *dikaios*" (14:13–14). The RSV translates *dikaios* as "just": "you will be repaid at the resurrection of the just."

In present-day English, "righteousness" is by no means a synonym of "justice"; so it makes a difference how one translates. Our English word *righteousness* comes from the Germanic *recht*. The noun *righteousness* and the adjective *righteous* belong, of course, to standard English. But nowadays they are seldom used outside of religious talk by Christians; in ordinary affairs one seldom hears someone described as "righteous." When someone is described in ordinary affairs as "righteous," the idea is that he is someone who is fastidiously concerned with his own moral rectitude. The word has come to suggest self-righteousness.

In present-day religious talk by Christians, "righteousness" has acquired a quite different meaning. It has come to mean *being right with God*, this being understood as a matter of the inner self. Being right with God in one's inner self does, of course, have consequences for how one treats one's fellows. But righteousness as such is understood as a matter of the heart. When Christians come across the word *righteousness* in English translations of the New Testament, that's how they typically understand it: being right with God in one's inner self.

Obviously they mean something different when they attribute righteousness to God; God's righteousness cannot consist of being right with God. In present-day Christian religious talk, "righteousness" when applied to God is typically understood as referring to God's retributive justice. God's "righteous anger" is God's anger at wrongdoing.

Given that both of the present-day meanings of *righteous* as applied to human beings are very different from the meaning of *just*, and that both of the present-day meanings of *righteousness* are very different from the meaning of *justice*, why do English translations of the New Testament typically translate the *dik*-stem words as "righteous," "righteousness," and so forth, whereas in English translations of Plato those same words are almost always translated as "just," "justice," and so forth?

One obvious explanation to be considered is that the meaning of the *dik*-stem words changed over the centuries between Plato and Jesus, and that the translators are reflecting this change. Here's the idea: whereas in Plato's day the meaning of the noun *dikaiosynē* was "justice," its dominant meaning at the time and place of the writing of the New Testament had come to be what we now call "righteousness." It had not entirely lost its old meaning, however; it could still be used to refer to justice. Accordingly, to determine, in a given case, whether the word is being used with its dominant meaning of "being right with God in one's inner self," or whether it is being used with its older, now subdominant, meaning of "justice," one has to consider what is being said and the context in which it is said. Our translators have made the judgment that, most of the time, content and context establish that what is meant is being right with God in one's inner self.

It's possible, of course, that *dikaiosynē* had indeed changed meaning in just this way, so that whereas at the time and place of the writing of the New Testament it usually means, when applied to human beings, being right with God in one's inner self, or perhaps being a person of moral rectitude; it could also still be used to mean justice. Since I am not a scholar of Greek, I cannot render a judgment on the matter. Nonetheless, let me be so bold as to offer an alternative suggestion that seems to me more plausible.

Start with the action of *acting justly* (*doing justice*). What I have called the Principle of Correlatives tells us that one who acts justly does what one ought to do. In standard present-day English, a near-synonym of "doing what one ought to do" is "doing the right thing." Acting justly is doing the right thing.

If we act justly, if we do the right thing, then *justice* in our relationships will be the result. Justice in our relationships results from our acting justly; it results from our doing the right thing.

Note next that some people act justly on occasion while others do so habitually. The habit of acting justly, of doing the right thing, is an aspect of the character of the latter sort of person; it's a character trait. We have no word, in standard idiomatic present-day English, for this character trait. Our word *courageous* refers to the character trait of those persons who habitually act courageously; our word *wisdom* refers to the character trait of those persons who habitually act wisely; our word *prudence* refers to the character trait of those persons who habitually act prudently; and so forth. But we have no word in present-day idiomatic English for the character trait of those persons who habitually act justly, for those who habitually do the right thing. Perhaps *righteousness* was once that word; that would go some way toward explaining why translators of the New Testament so commonly use it to translate *dikaiosynē*. But *righteousness* no longer picks out that character trait. It picks out the character trait of being right with God in one's inner self. Or when used in ordinary affairs, it picks out the character trait of moral rectitude. And both of those character traits are very different from the character trait of habitually acting justly, of habitually doing the right thing.

I have singled out three distinct, but closely related, phenomena: (1) a certain way of acting—namely, doing the right thing, acting justly; (2) the sort of relationship that results from so acting—namely, just relationships, relationships characterized by justice; (3) the character trait of habitually doing the just or the right thing. I think it not unlikely that *dikaiosynē* in the New Testament can refer to any one of these three phenomena; it is, in that way, ambiguous. In the next chapter we will look at some passages to see how this idea works out.

Before we turn to that, however, let me make a brief comment about meaning and translation in the Old Testament. There we find the pair *mishpat* and *tsedeqa* almost always translated as "justice and righteousness." The term *mishpat* comes from the law courts and clearly means justice; the root meaning of *tsedeqa* is straight, correct, upright.

Scholars have long discussed and argued over how we should understand the pair. Quite clearly the terms are not synonyms, but *mishpat* and *tsedeqa* must have some intimate relation to each other. The distinctions I drew above, between (1) actions that are right or just, (2) justice as characterizing our social relationships when we act justly, and (3) the character trait of those who are disposed to act justly, suggests some possibilities.

Suppose that the term *mishpat* refers to the second of these, that characteristic of our social relationships that we call, in English, "justice." That leaves it open for the term *tsedeqa* to refer either to just or right actions, or to that character trait of persons that disposes them to right or just actions. Context and content would have to determine, in each case, with which meaning the term was being used. If this suggestion is correct, then *mishpat* and *tsedeqa* will in each case be intimately related while yet the terms have different meanings.

The RSV translation of Isaiah 32:16–17 reads as follows:

> Justice will dwell in the wilderness,
> > and righteousness abide in the fruitful field.
> And the effect of righteousness will be peace,
> > and the result of righteousness, quietness and trust for ever.

The Hebrew word translated as "justice" is *mishpat* and the Hebrew word translated as "righteousness" is *tsedeqa*.

Obviously *tsedeqa* does not here mean what "righteousness" has come to mean in Christian religious contexts—namely, being right with God in one's inner self. Might it mean moral rectitude? Perhaps; but to describe the character trait of moral rectitude as "abiding in the fruitful field" strikes me as strange. It is much more natural to describe doing justice as abiding in the fruitful field.

> Justice will dwell in the wilderness
> > and [doing justice] will abide in the fruitful field.
> And the effect of [doing justice] will be peace,
> > and the result of [doing justice], quietness and trust forever.

On this reading, *mishpat* and *tsedeqa* are intimately connected, but the terms are not synonymous.[1]

The RSV translation of Amos 5:24 reads as follows:

> Let justice roll down like waters,
> and righteousness like an ever-flowing stream.

To ask that the character trait of moral rectitude, or any character trait, roll down like an ever-flowing stream, strikes me again as strange; it is much more natural to ask that doing what is right roll down like an ever-flowing stream.

> Let justice roll down like waters,
> and [doing what is right] like an ever-flowing stream.

---

1. The Jerusalem Bible translates the passage as follows:
> In the wilderness justice will come to live
> and integrity in the fertile land;
> integrity will bring peace [shalom],
> justice give lasting security.

❖ 16 ❖

More about Justice
in the New Testament

In one of the Beatitudes, as we find them in Matthew, we read, "Blessed are those who are persecuted for the sake of *dikaiosynē*, for theirs is the kingdom of heaven" (5:10). The Revised Standard Version, along with most other English versions, translates *dikaiosynē* as "righteousness": "Blessed are those who are persecuted for righteousness' sake." This is implausible. People are not persecuted for wanting to be right with God in their inner selves; neither are they persecuted for being persons of moral rectitude. It's those who do justice and seek to right injustice who get under people's skin and are persecuted. Jesus is blessing those who are persecuted for doing what is right—for doing justice and seeking to right injustice. The Jerusalem Bible translates the beatitude this way: "Happy those who are persecuted in the cause of right."

Another of the Beatitudes in Matthew's version reads thus: "Blessed are those who hunger and thirst for *dikaiosynē*, for they shall be satisfied" (5:6). The RSV, along with most other English versions, translates *dikaiosynē* as "righteousness": "Blessed are those who hunger and thirst for righteousness." Is that correct? Is Jesus blessing those who hunger and thirst for being right with God in their inner selves? Or is he perhaps blessing those who hunger and thirst for moral rectitude? That's not impossible. But if we translate the occurrence of *dikaiosynē* in the other beatitude with "justice," and translate this one with "righteousness," we conceal from English readers the linguistic connection in the Greek. Jesus is blessing those who hunger and thirst for justice, for what is right. Once again the Jerusalem Bible gets it right: "Happy those who hunger and thirst for what is right."

In Matthew 3:15–17 we read about Jesus's insistence, over John the Baptist's protests, that John baptize him. Jesus says, "Let it be so now; for thus it is fitting for us to fulfill all *dikaiosynē*" (v. 15). The RSV, along with most other English versions, translates *dikaiosynē* as "righteousness": "Let it be so now; for thus it is fitting for us to fulfill all righteousness." Given what "righteousness" has come to mean, this makes no sense. It makes no sense to say that being right with God in one's inner self will be fulfilled by John's baptism of Jesus; neither does it make any sense to say that moral rectitude will be fulfilled.

How, then, should the passage be translated? Well, recall from an earlier chapter Matthew's identification of Jesus: "he shall proclaim justice [*krisis*] to the Gentiles" (12:18) and "he brings justice [*krisis*] to victory" (12:20). It is justice that Jesus has come to bring about and that John's baptism of him will somehow fulfill.

In Matthew 6:33 we read, "Seek first your heavenly Father's kingdom and his *dikaiosynē*, and all these things shall be yours as well." The RSV, along with most other English translations, translates *dikaiosynē* as "righteousness": "Seek first [your heavenly Father's] kingdom and his righteousness." Is that correct? Was Jesus telling us to seek our heavenly Father's kingdom and being right with God in our inner selves? Alternatively, was he telling us to seek our heavenly Father's kingdom and moral rectitude? I doubt it. Jesus's listeners and Matthew's original readers, steeped as they were in the Scriptures of the Old Testament, would automatically have connected God's kingdom with the doing of justice and with the righting of injustice.

Jesus is telling us to seek our heavenly Father's kingdom and the justice that its coming will bring.

In chapter 14 we looked at Nygren's interpretation of Jesus's parable of the laborers in the vineyard. To the day-laborers that the landowner found standing around idle in the marketplace around the third hour of the day, he says, "Go into the vineyard . . . , and whatever is *dikaios* I will give you" (Matt. 20:4). The RSV translates the adjective *dikaios* as "right": "whatever is right, I will give you." Later the owner says to one of the grumblers, "Friend, I am not treating you *adikos*" (v. 13). The RSV translates this as, "Friend, I am doing you no wrong." These translations seem to me correct. I will pay you whatever is right, says the landowner to those he hired at the third hour—that is, I will pay you whatever is just. (The Jerusalem Bible translates *dikaios* as "a fair wage.") I am doing you no wrong, he says to the grumblers—that is, I am not treating you unjustly. (The Jerusalem Bible translates it as "I am not being unjust to you.")

The parable of the great assize, as it was traditionally called, requires a somewhat more extensive treatment. In old English, an *assize* was a session of court. Traditionally the parable has been regarded as the grand charter of Christian hospitality and charity. In welcoming the stranger, we are extending hospitality to Jesus; in nursing the sick, we are having compassion on Jesus. In the translation of the NRSV the parable reads as follows:

> When the Son of Man comes in all his glory, and all the angels with him, then he will sit on the throne of his glory. All the nations will be gathered before him, and he will separate people one from another as a shepherd separates the sheep from the goats, and he will put the sheep at his right hand and the goats at the left. Then the king will say to those at his right hand, "Come, you that are blessed by my Father, inherit the kingdom prepared for you from the foundation of the world; for I was hungry and you gave me food, I was thirsty and you gave me something to drink, I was a stranger and you welcomed me, I was naked and you gave me clothing, I was sick and you took care of me, I was in prison and you visited me." Then the righteous will answer him, "Lord, when was

it that we saw you hungry and gave you food, or thirsty and gave you something to drink? And when was it that we saw you a stranger and welcomed you, or naked and gave you clothing? And when was it that we saw you sick or in prison and visited you?" And the king will answer them, "Truly I tell you, just as you did it to one of the least of these who are members of my family, you did it to me." Then he will say to those at his left hand, "You that are accursed, depart from me into the eternal fire prepared for the devil and his angels; for I was hungry and you gave me no food, I was thirsty and you gave me nothing to drink, I was a stranger and you did not welcome me, naked and you did not give me clothing, sick and in prison and you did not visit me." Then they also will answer, "Lord, when was it that we saw you hungry or thirsty or a stranger or naked or sick or in prison, and did not take care of you?" Then he will answer them, "Truly I tell you, just as you did not do it to one of the least of these, you did not do it to me." And these will go away into eternal punishment, but the righteous into eternal life. (Matt. 25:31–46)

The word *righteous* occurs twice in this translation. The blessing has been announced and the reason given: when Jesus was hungry we gave him food, when he was thirsty we gave him something to drink, when he was a stranger we welcomed him, when he was naked we gave him clothes, and so on. Then our English text says that "the righteous" reply, "Lord, when was it that we saw you hungry. . . ." Later our English text says that those on the king's left go away into eternal punishment but "the righteous" enter into eternal life. In both cases, the Greek word translated as "righteous" is the adjective *dikaios*.

Is this translation correct? Well, clearly Jesus is not identifying those on his right hand as right with God in their inner selves; in the context of the parable that makes no sense. Is he then perhaps identifying them as those of moral rectitude? That is essentially how the Jerusalem Bible understands him; it translates both occurrences of *dikaios* as "virtuous."

But notice the examples Jesus gives of *dikaios* action: giving food to the hungry, giving water to the thirsty, welcoming the stranger, giving clothing to the naked, taking care of the sick, visiting the prisoner.

Now recall the examples of doing justice in the passage from Isaiah (61:1–2) that Jesus adapted in the synagogue: bringing good tidings to the afflicted, binding up the brokenhearted, proclaiming liberty to the captives, opening the prison to those who are bound. Recall also the examples of doing justice in the passage I quoted that occurs a few chapters earlier in Isaiah (58:6–7): loosing the bonds of wickedness, undoing the thongs of the yoke, letting the oppressed go free, sharing one's bread with the hungry, bringing the homeless poor into one's house, covering the naked.

I submit that Jesus's listeners would have heard his parable as echoing these passages, and that Matthew's original readers would have read the parable that same way. The parable is about doing justice, about doing the right thing. It is *the just*—those who have done the right thing—who are puzzled and say, "Lord, when was it that we saw you hungry. . . ." It is *the just* who enter eternal life. This is the grand charter for doing justice and seeking to right injustice. And incidentally, what we see here is that the Old Testament's preferential option for the vulnerable is carried over into the New Testament.

More could be said about the translation of the *dik*-stem words in Matthew's Gospel; and I have said nothing at all about their translation in the other Gospels. But let me move on to Paul's Letter to the Romans. Near the beginning of his letter (1:16–17) Paul states his major theme: "For I am not ashamed of the gospel; it is the power of God for salvation to everyone who has faith, to the Jew first and also to the Greek. For in it the *dikaiosynē* of God is revealed through faith for faith; as it is written, 'He who through faith is *dikaios* shall live.'" In the RSV and almost all other English translations, *dikaiosynē* is translated as "righteousness" and *dikaios* as "righteous."

Very many if not most of those who hear that the theme of Paul's letter is God's righteousness will assume that the theme is God's righteous anger at wrongdoers. And Paul does indeed speak immediately about the wrath of God against all ungodliness and wickedness. But rather than just going with our assumptions, let's look at what Paul actually says.

The brief phrase in 1:16, "to the Jew first and also to the Greek," hints at a theme that runs throughout the first eleven chapters. There is no distinction between Jews and Gentiles with respect to their sinfulness, hence there is also none with respect to God's judgment on them. But so too there is no distinction between Jews and Gentiles with respect to God's offer of justification. God offers justification on the same terms to everybody; all that is required for the reception of the offer is faith, and faith is available to everybody. "Since God is one . . . he will justify the circumcised on the ground of their faith and the uncircumcised through their faith" (3:30). "There is no distinction" (3:22; repeated in 10:12). "God shows no partiality" (2:11).

This theme of God's impartiality was not an innovation on Paul's part. In Deuteronomy Moses declares to Israel that the Lord your God "is not partial and takes no bribe. He executes justice for the fatherless and the widow, and loves the sojourner, giving him food and clothing" (10:17–18). In 2 Chronicles 19:7 the Judean king Jehoshaphat is reported as declaring that "there is no perversion of justice with the LORD our God, or partiality, or taking bribes." And Job says of God that he "shows no partiality to princes, nor regards the rich more than the poor, for they are all the work of his hands" (34:19). Israel's judges are to imitate God and "not be partial in judgment." They are to "hear the small and the great alike" (Deut. 1:17).

In an episode reported in all three Synoptic Gospels, the term "no partiality" is used to capture the pattern of Jesus's engagement with those with whom he came into contact: he showed "no partiality." The episode is the one in which some opponents of Jesus tried to trap him with the famous trick question about the morality of paying taxes to the Roman emperor. In all three narrations the interrogator prefaced his question with a reference to Jesus's reputation. Let me quote Matthew's version: "Teacher, we know that you are sincere, and teach the way of God in accordance with truth, and show deference to no one; for you do not regard people with partiality" (22:16 NRSV; cf. Mark 12:14; Luke 20:21). The reference to Jesus's reputation for teaching the truth is flattery; the reference to his reputation for showing deference to no one and not regarding anyone with partiality is preparation for setting the trap. How far is Jesus willing to go in showing deference to no one? Is he willing to go all the way up to the emperor?

This theme of no partiality is picked up in the book of Acts. A visionary trance leads Peter to conclude that he must give up his Jewish particularism. "I truly understand," he says, "that God shows no partiality, but in every nation anyone who fears him and does justice [*dikaiosynē*] is acceptable to him" (10:34–35 NRSV, modified).[1]

In short, Paul's Letter to the Romans both carries forward the Old Testament theme of God as not showing partiality and is a dense and extended meditation on the theological significance of Jesus's actions and Peter's vision.

Now for the question. Suppose that in one's distribution of some good, one shows no partiality. Surely that is an example of acting justly. Rather than repudiating the Old Testament theme of the justice of God, Paul gives that theme a new application. The love of God, as exhibited in God's offer of justification, is a love that is just. Just love. The Jerusalem Bible gets it right. Here is how it translates Paul's statement of his theme: "For I am not ashamed of the Good News: it is the power of God saving all who have faith—Jews first, but Greeks as well—since this is what reveals the justice of God to us."[2]

My point, in looking at the English translations of a few of the *dik*-stem words in the New Testament, has been to show that our English translations conceal from us the prominence of the theme of justice in the New Testament. English translations of the New Testament don't mention justice very often; that helps to explain why a good many readers of English translations believe that justice has been supplanted in the New Testament.

---

1. For "does justice" the NRSV has "does what is right."

2. But I am baffled as to why the Jerusalem Bible then goes on to translate as follows the line that concludes Paul's statement of his theme: "The upright man finds life through faith." Why not the *just* man, or the man *who does right*?

❖ 17 ❖

Justice and Love

The common view, that love supplants justice in the New Testament, has to be rejected. The New Testament believer is called, as was the Old Testament Israelite, to do justice and seek to right injustice. But if love does not supplant justice, how then are love and justice related?

Recall that Nygren presented his concept of love—as self-sacrificial generosity that pays no attention to what justice requires—as an interpretation of what Jesus meant when he attributed love for us to God and enjoined us to love our neighbor as ourselves. It is time to consider for ourselves what Jesus meant by *agapē*.

All three of the Synoptic Gospels report the episode in which Jesus enunciated the two love commands (Matt. 22:34–40; Mark 12:28–34; Luke 10:25–37). The episode is described a bit differently in the three Gospels. But in their report of the two commands themselves, there are only slight rhetorical differences—with two exceptions. Mark reports Jesus as introducing the first command with the Shema: "Hear, O Israel: the Lord our God, the Lord is one." And Matthew reports Jesus as saying that the second command is like the first.

The first command says that we are to love God with our whole being. Nygren saw this as posing a difficulty for his interpretation of love as self-sacrificial gratuitous generosity. Treating God with gratuitous generosity seemed to him impossible. So with the courage of his convictions he concluded that Jesus and the New Testament writers were speaking loosely when they said that we are to love God. What they meant, strictly speaking, was that we are to have *faith* in God.

What, then, are we to make of Jesus's statement, in Matthew, that the second command is like the first? Given Nygren's interpretation of the two commandments, the second is quite unlike the first. Faith is not at all the same as self-sacrificial gratuitous benevolence. I am not aware that Nygren ever addressed this question.

The second command says that one is to love one's neighbor as oneself. The rhetorical structure of the command is the familiar *just as . . . so also* structure. Just as you love yourself, so also, love your neighbor. You love yourself, right? Love your neighbor as well. The command presupposes not only the actuality but the legitimacy of self-love and enjoins us to love not only ourselves but our neighbors as well. Of course some people do not love themselves—not very much, anyway; and love of self is always distorted, sometimes severely so.

Love of self is obviously not self-sacrificial gratuitous benevolence. Karl Barth often described agape as "being for the other." But love of self is being for *oneself*, not being for *the other*. In this case, Nygren did not resort to saying that Jesus must have been speaking loosely. Instead he emphatically declared that Christianity is opposed to all forms of self-love. I am not aware of any place in which he asked how this position can be squared with the fact that the second love command takes for granted not only the actuality but the legitimacy of self-love.

Now for a point that is more important for our purposes than either of the two preceding points. The two love commands are not just statements of the essence or heart of Torah. They are quotations from the Torah. The first is a quotation from Deuteronomy 6; the second is a quotation from Leviticus 19. The thought comes to mind that if we look at the context in which these two commandments occur in the Torah, perhaps that will illuminate their meaning in the Torah. Context doesn't always illuminate meaning, but often it does. Suppose that it does in this case. It seems likely that Jesus and his interrogators would have understood the commands as having the same meaning that they had in the Torah. It's possible that they understood them differently, but the burden of proof lies on the person who holds that they did. On this occasion, let's confine ourselves to looking at the context in which the second command occurs in the Torah.

Moses is delivering to Israel the divine law code that is nowadays often called by scholars the "Holiness Code," to distinguish it from the "Book of the Covenant" in Exodus and from the "Deuteronomic laws" in the book of Deuteronomy. The context extends over several chapters. It will be sufficient for our purposes here to quote just a few of the immediately preceding verses.

> You shall not oppress your neighbor or rob him. The wages of a hired servant shall not remain with you all night until the morning. . . . You shall do no injustice in judgment; you shall not be partial to the poor or defer to the great, but in righteousness shall you judge your neighbor. You shall not go up and down as a slanderer among your people, and you shall not stand forth against the life of your neighbor. . . . You shall not hate your brother in your heart, but you shall reason with your neighbor, lest you bear sin because of him. You shall not take vengeance or bear any grudge against the sons of your own people, but you shall love your neighbor as yourself. I am the LORD. (Lev. 19:13–18)

What we have here is a number of more or less detailed injunctions concluding with the love command. A question that comes to mind is whether that final command, love your neighbor as yourself, should be regarded as just one injunction among many. That is not how Jesus and his interrogators regarded it; it was for them the heart of the Torah. And that remains how the Jewish tradition interprets it. The love command is the generalized summation of what has preceded.

We are to read it as if it were prefaced with the words "in short." "In short, love your neighbor as yourself."

Now for the point relevant to our present concerns. Love and justice are not pitted against each other. To the contrary: treating one's neighbor justly is cited as an example of loving one's neighbor. Just action is an example of love. The love that Jesus enjoins on us for our neighbors is not to be understood as sheer gratuitous benevolence that pays no attention to what justice requires. If that is how we have understood New Testament love, we have to rethink our understanding so that love incorporates justice.

How do we do that? Over the past several years, when I have talked about these matters, a response I have often received is that in Scripture love, justice, righteousness, and so forth are all basically the same. The formula that is over and over offered up is that all of these have to do with *right relationships*. I do not know where this idea originated, but it has now become a commonplace. When I ask what is meant by "right" in this phrase, I never get a clarifying answer. Are right relationships simply *good* relationships? Are they *just* relationships? What are they?

This strategy of rubbing out the distinctions should be rejected. I take it as fundamental to the biblical understanding of forgiveness that even the repentant wrongdoer cannot claim a right to be forgiven; he cannot claim that justice requires that he be forgiven. Forgiveness is always an act of grace, of love. Nygren was right about that. But if one blurs love and justice together into *right relationships*, it becomes impossible to make that point. To make the point one has to distinguish between love and justice.

Further, Paul's overarching argument in his Letter to the Romans, as I argued in the preceding chapter, is that in offering justification to Jews and Gentiles alike, God is acting justly. God's love is just love. The book of Romans is about the justice of God's love. But this point too cannot be made if love and justice are blurred together into something called "right relationships."

So once again: How can we understand love so that treating a person as justice requires is an example of loving that person?

Recall my claim that justice is grounded in rights; and recall my suggestion that to understand what a right is we must distinguish between, on the one hand, how well or poorly a person's life is going and, on the other hand, the worth or value of that person herself. A truly admirable person may find that her life is going poorly; these are the Jobs of the world. Conversely, a person whose life is going very well may not be an admirable person; this gives rise to the ancient complaint, why do the wicked prosper?

Rights, as I understand them, are constituted of an interweaving of these two phenomena, that of how well or poorly a person's life is going (her well-being), and that of the worth or dignity of the person herself. Specifically, one has a right to the life-good of being treated a certain way just in case not being treated that way would constitute being treated in a way that does not befit one's worth. To deprive a person of her right to the life-good of being treated a certain way is to treat that person with under-respect. An ethical framework that works only with the idea of life-goods, and not also with the idea of the worth or dignity of persons, cannot, in my view, give an adequate account of rights, and hence not an adequate account of justice.

Here, then, is my suggestion as to how the love that Jesus attributes to God and enjoins on us should be understood. Such love seeks to advance the good of the other. The good of the other (and of oneself) has two dimensions: the dimension of the well-being of the other, and the dimension of respect for the worth of the other. Love attends to both dimensions—not just to the former. Love seeks to promote the well-being of the other, but love also sees to it that the worth of the other is respected. Love does not promote the well-being of someone at the cost of treating that person or anyone else in a way that does not befit his or her worth or dignity. Promoting the well-being of someone at the cost of wronging someone is impermissible.

What makes paternalistic benevolence wrong is that the agent seeks to advance the good of the recipient while failing to pay due respect to his or her worth. That's what I saw happening when I first visited South Africa: paternalistic benevolence riding roughshod over the dignity of the so-called blacks and coloreds. Their dignity, and what respect for their dignity required, never entered the purview of those who defended apartheid.

Do we have a word in English for this two-dimensional sort of love: love that both seeks to advance the well-being of the other and sees to it that she is treated with due respect? I think we do. It's the word *care*—"care" in the sense of caring *about* someone, not in the sense of caring *for* someone. When one cares about someone, one seeks both to advance her well-being and to ensure that she is treated with due respect for her worth—that she is not demeaned, not treated with under-respect. When I see someone causing another person needless pain, thereby diminishing her well-being, I get angry. And when I see someone demeaning another person, I also get angry—even if, in the course of demeaning her, they shower her with all sorts of good things. In both cases, my anger is a manifestation of my care. It must be conceded that "care" is not a strong word; but so far as I can see, it's the best we have in English.

When Jesus said, "Love your neighbor as yourself," he was not enjoining us to treat the neighbor with self-sacrificial, justice-blind benevolence. He was enjoining us to care about the neighbor. It may be that only in a minimal way can I advance the well-being of my enemy. But I can always treat him with due respect for his worth, and in that way care about him.

Nygren and Niebuhr thought that in this conflictual world of ours, self-sacrificing gratuitous benevolence might be well formed in all respects while nonetheless perpetrating or abetting injustice. I suggest that benevolence that perpetrates injustice is *malformed* care. It exhibits one dimension of well-formed care, the benevolence dimension; but it lacks the other dimension, the respect dimension.

I have been assuming that all human beings do have worth. Some human beings, let's face it, are despicable. They spread pain and suffering all about them; they demean their fellow human beings, treat them like dirt. I remember a newspaper report about a man in Cleveland who was convicted and imprisoned some years back for rape but then released and who, after his release, killed at least eleven women and buried them in various places around his house. This is an "enemy" if ever there was one. Our natural impulse is to feel nothing but anger toward him, seething anger. But Jesus tells us that we are to love him. What can this possibly mean? What it means, I suggest, is that even if we subject him to the hard treatment of punishment, as we should, we must not demean him; we must treat him in accord with his worth.

He has no worth, someone says. He's nothing but scum. Not so, says Scripture, you're wrong about that. He too bears the image of God, and even to him God extends his offer of justification. These give him worth. There's nothing he or others can do to get rid of such worth. I will have more to say about this shortly.

I hold that every interpretation of *agapē* in the New Testament should aim at being a *unified* interpretation, in the sense that it is the same form of love that Jesus attributes to God for us, that Jesus enjoins on us for God and neighbor, and that Jesus assumes we have for ourselves. We may fail to achieve such a unified interpretation; but that is what we should aim at.

We saw that Nygren's interpretation falls far short of this goal. After explaining what he takes agapic love to be—namely, self-sacrificial benevolence that takes no account of what justice requires—he observes that God cannot be an object of such love. He concludes that Jesus was speaking loosely when he said that we should love God agapically; what he meant, speaking strictly, is that we should have faith in God. And as to love for oneself, Nygren holds that Christianity rejects all forms of self-love.

How does my suggestion, that we understand agapic love as *care*, fare by the test I have suggested? It's obvious on the face of it that one can care both about oneself and about one's neighbor, and that God can care about us. What is not obvious is that one can care about God. Some will wonder whether there is not, in fact, something theologically inept about saying that one cares about God. To care about someone presupposes that they are vulnerable, does it not—vulnerable to impairments to their well-being, vulnerable to being treated in a way that does not befit their worth? But is God vulnerable in these ways? The traditional doctrine of divine impassibility holds that God is not.

The psalmist enjoins the peoples of the earth to "ascribe to the LORD the glory due his name" (96:8), the assumption being, obviously, that often they do not. And Jesus taught us to pray that God's name be hallowed, the assumption being, again, that often it is not. In short, the biblical writers present God as being wronged; we fail to treat God as befits God's worth. And they present God as both pleased and angered by how we treat God. God is presented as vulnerable in exactly the ways presupposed by saying that we are to care about God.

Even for those who take Scripture as authoritative, however, it does not follow, from the fact that this is how Scripture presents God, that this is how God is; we have to allow for metaphors, anthropomorphisms, and the like. In some passages God is presented as a rock; God is not literally a rock. What is the case, however, is that the burden of proof lies on those who think that some particular aspect of the biblical presentation of God should not be taken literally.

I have argued elsewhere that that burden of proof has not been successfully borne by those who hold that God is not vulnerable in the ways described.[1] Of course there are fundamental ways in which God is not vulnerable: God is not vulnerable to being put out of existence, God is not vulnerable to limitations on God's power. But God is vulnerable to our wronging God, and thus vulnerable to being angered.

1. See my "Is God Disturbed by What Transpires in Human Affairs?" in my *Inquiring about God: Selected Essays*, vol. 1, ed. Terence Cuneo (Cambridge: Cambridge University Press, 2010), 223–38.

❖ 18 ❖

Justice, Love, and Shalom

One of the areas of philosophy in which I was teaching and writing at the time I attended the conference in Potchefstroom was philosophy of art. On the way to the conference I stopped in Nairobi, Kenya, to visit a former student and her husband, a professor of philosophy at the University of Nairobi. On a weekend they drove me north up a valley lush with coffee and tea plantings to his home village of Karatina. On the way we stopped at a mission compound whose director they knew. The buildings of the compound were some of the most shabby and squalid structures I have ever seen: they were poorly built and had peeling paint, and there was dirt and refuse everywhere. What these buildings said, loud and clear, was that aesthetic decency doesn't count when you're in the business of saving souls; ugliness is okay. The image came to mind of the gorgeous hills of the valley vomiting out this monstrosity that had been forced down their throat. I have sometimes used this example when arguing for the importance of beauty in our lives—not complicated elaborate beauty, but simple beauty, aesthetically decent surroundings.

On the plane back from Potchefstroom I began to worry that my life was falling irreparably into fragments. I loved philosophy. I loved the arts. I had designed the house in which we lived; my wife and I had been collecting graphic art prints; I loved music. Through various experiences I had come to care deeply about liturgy. Now justice was on my agenda. These loves were pulling me in different directions, tearing me apart. Did they cohere in some way of which I was unaware? Or did I have to put up with living a fragmented existence?

Some time after I returned I was struck by the prominence of the concept of *shalom* in the poetic and prophetic literature of the Old Testament. In the Septuagint (the original Greek translation of the Old Testament), the Hebrew word *shalom* is translated with the Greek word *eirēnē*. This same word, *eirēnē*, occurs a good many times in the Greek original of the New Testament.

In most English translations of the Bible, the Hebrew word *shalom* and the Greek word *eirēnē* are translated as "peace." And shalom does indeed require peace. It is shalom when

> the wolf shall dwell with the lamb,
>   and the leopard shall lie down with the kid,
> and the calf and the lion and the fatling together,
>   and a little child shall lead them.
> The cow and the bear shall feed,
>   their young shall lie down together,
>   and the lion shall eat straw like the ox.
> The suckling child shall play over the hole of the asp,
>   and the weaned child shall put his hand on the adder's den.
> They shall not hurt or destroy
>   in all my holy mountain. (Isa. 11:6–9)

But shalom goes beyond peace, beyond the absence of hostility. A nation may be at peace and yet be miserable in its poverty. Shalom is not just peace but *flourishing*, flourishing in all dimensions of our existence—in our relation to God, in our relation to our fellow human beings, in our relation to ourselves, in our relation to creation in general. Both the cry for justice by the so-called blacks and coloreds in Potchefstroom and the attempt of the Kenyan hills to vomit out the monstrosity of the mission compound were calls for shalom and laments for its absence. Beauty, liturgy, justice, the sort of understanding that philosophy can yield—these are fundamentally united in that each is a dimension of shalom.

Shalom incorporates flourishing in our relation to God. When the prophets speak of shalom, they foresee a day when human beings will no longer flee God down the corridors of time, a day when they will no longer turn in those corridors to defy their divine pursuer.[1] They foresee a day when the human community flourishes in its love and service of God. In the words of the prophet Isaiah,

> The mountain of the house of the LORD
> > shall be established as the highest of the mountains,
> > and shall be raised above the hills;
> and all the nations shall flow to it,
> > and many peoples shall come, and say:
> "Come, let us go up to the mountain of the LORD,
> > to the house of the God of Jacob;
> that he may teach us his ways
> > and that we may walk in his paths." (Isa. 2:2–3)

Shalom also incorporates flourishing in our relations with one another. Shalom is absent when society is a collection of individuals each out to make his or her own way in the world. And it is absent wherever there is injustice, wherever people are wronged.

One can be wronged even if one doesn't know that one is, or knows that one is but doesn't mind. Shalom is absent even if those who are wronged feel content with their lot in life. Shalom would have been absent from South Africa before the revolution *even if* all the so-called blacks and coloreds had been content with apartheid—which, of course, they were not. Shalom would have been absent from the United States before emancipation *even if* all the slaves had been content in their state of slavery—which, of course, they were not. Genuine flourishing is not just feeling good. Genuine flourishing is present only when we no longer wrong and oppress one another. Shalom has

---

1. I am alluding here to Francis Thompson's poem "The Hound of Heaven."

justice as its ground floor. Shalom goes beyond justice, but shalom is never less than justice. Isaiah declares that there will be shalom when

> justice will dwell in the wilderness,
>> and [doing what is right] abide in the fruitful field.
> And the effect of [doing what is right] will be [shalom],
>> and the result of [doing what is right], quietness and trust
>> for ever. (Isa. 32:16–17)

Finally, shalom incorporates flourishing in our relation to our physical surroundings. Shalom is present when we—bodily creatures, not disembodied souls—flourish in our relation to the earth and its creatures, flourish in our physical labor and its results, flourish in our bodies. In speaking of shalom, Isaiah foresees a day when the Lord will prepare "for all peoples a feast of rich food, a feast of well-aged wines, of rich food filled with marrow, of well-aged wines strained clear" (Isa. 25:6 NRSV). He foresees the day when the people "will abide in [habitations of shalom], in secure dwellings, and in quiet resting places" (Isa. 32:18).

I have already cited that best known of all shalom passages, the one in which Isaiah describes the anticipated shalom with a flourish of images of harmony—harmony among the animals, harmony between human beings and animals: "Then the wolf shall dwell with the lamb. . . ." That passage is introduced with these words:

> There shall come forth a shoot from the stump of Jesse,
>> and a branch shall grow out of his roots.
> And the Spirit of the LORD shall rest upon him,
>> the spirit of wisdom and understanding,
>> the spirit of counsel and might,
>> the spirit of knowledge and the fear of the LORD.
> And his delight shall be in the fear of the LORD. (Isa. 11:1–3)

Those of us who are Christians believe that the shoot of which Isaiah spoke is he of whom the angels sang in celebration of his birth, "Glory to God in the highest, and on earth shalom [Greek, *eirēnē*] among [those] with whom he is well pleased" (Luke 2:14). We believe that he is the one of whom the priest Zechariah said that he will "guide our feet into the way of [shalom]" (Luke 1:79). We believe that he is the one of whom Simeon said, "Lord, now lettest thou thy servant depart in [shalom], according to thy word" (Luke 2:29). We believe that he is the one of whom Peter said that it was by him that God preached "good news of [shalom]" to Israel (Acts 10:36). We believe that he is the one of whom Paul, speaking as a Jew to the Gentiles, said that "he came and preached [shalom] to you who were far off and [shalom] to those who were near" (Eph. 2:17). We believe that he is Jesus Christ, whom Isaiah called the "Prince of [Shalom]" (Isa. 9:6). It was this Jesus who said to the apostles, in his farewell discourse, "[Shalom] I leave with you; my [shalom] I give to you; not as the world gives do I give to you. Let not your hearts be troubled" (John 14:27).

Much more could be said by way of articulating the biblical understanding of *shalom/eirēnē*. But this is enough for our purposes here. Let me now note that shalom is intimately connected with the love for one's neighbors that Jesus enjoins on us. To love one's neighbors as one loves oneself is to seek the shalom of one's neighbors as one seeks one's own shalom. It is to seek the flourishing of the human community. And it is because shalom incorporates justice that biblical love incorporates justice. Shalom goes beyond justice. But shalom never falls short of justice. That's why it is that well-formed care never falls short of justice.

In an earlier chapter I cited the view, common in certain evangelical quarters, that it is not the business of Christians to seek justice; justice is God's business. Our business is to love people and wait patiently for that day when God will bring about justice and vindicate those who were wronged. It is now clear how misguided this view is, in its pitting of love against justice. Love incorporates justice because shalom incorporates justice and love seeks the shalom of the community. The love that seeks shalom is both God's cause in the world and our calling. Though the full incursion of shalom into history will be divine gift and not merely human achievement, though its episodic incursion into our present lives also has a dimension of divine gift, nonetheless it is justice-in-shalom for which we are to work and struggle. We are not to stand around, hands folded, waiting for it to arrive. We are workers in God's cause. The *missio Dei* is our mission.

❖ 19 ❖

Does Scripture Imply a Right Order Conception of Justice?

It's time to return to Ambrose of Milan, Basil of Caesarea, and John Chrysostom. We found them saying that the extra clothes of the wealthy *belong to* the poor who have none and that their extra food *belongs to* those who have insufficient food. Though none of the three used a term that is a synonym of our term "a right," to say that something *belongs to* someone is to presuppose that the person has a right to it, a legitimate claim.

Ambrose, Basil, and John based their comments about the rights of the poor on their interpretation of Scripture. Were they overinterpreting? They would certainly not have been overinterpreting had they contented themselves with noting that Scripture says that justice requires coming to the aid of the poor. But they go beyond that. They presuppose that the poor have a *right* to clothing and to means of sustenance, a *natural* right. In so doing, were they perhaps reading their own views about justice into Scripture?

I have articulated and defended the view that justice is grounded in rights: our social relations are just when we are treated as we have a right to be treated. And I have defended the view that among our rights there are natural rights. These claims are controversial. Some who acknowledge the claims of justice deny that there are natural rights; they insist that whatever rights we have are all socially generated in one way or another. May it be that that was how the biblical writers implicitly thought about justice?

The question, let's be clear, is not whether the biblical writers employed the concept and terminology of natural rights; the question is whether, in what they said, they *presupposed* the existence of natural rights. They do on occasion speak of rights—birthrights, for example. But from what they explicitly say about these and other rights it's not clear—not clear to me, at least—whether they took them to be natural rights or socially conferred. Our question is not about the terminology of Scripture but about its implicit assumptions.

Christian Scripture does indeed imply and presuppose the existence of natural rights. Begin with God. Running throughout Christian Scripture is the assumption that God has rights with regard to us—a right to our obedience, a right to due acknowledgment of God's worth, and so forth. "Ascribe to the LORD the glory due his name," says the psalmist (96:8). These rights are natural; it is not by virtue of some human action that God has these rights. Of course they are not natural *human* rights; they are natural *divine* rights.

The assumption that God has a right to our praise and obedience underlies the assumption that God is acting justly when God punishes those who do not render him praise and obedience. It also underlies the declaration that God foregoes punishing the penitent wrongdoer and instead forgives. As we noted earlier, to forgive someone for what that person did to one presupposes that one has been wronged, deprived of something to which one had a right. If what was done amounted to no more than depriving one of something that one desired but not something to which one had a right, then regret would be the relevant response, not forgiveness. The declaration that God forgives the penitent wrongdoer implies that God was treated in a way that violated God's rights.

What, then, about human beings? Does Scripture imply or presuppose that human beings have natural rights? It does indeed. Scripture assumes that we have natural obligations toward our fellows. But if I have a natural obligation to my fellows, then, given the Principle of Correlatives, they have natural rights with regard to me. I am obligated not to murder my neighbor—whether or not this is the law of the land. But then my neighbor has the correlative right against me that I not murder him.

Ambrose, Basil, and John were not overinterpreting when, in commenting on Scripture, they presupposed the existence of natural rights.

Let's move on to a related issue. I began my discussion of the nature of justice by distinguishing between two fundamentally different ways of thinking about justice, the *right order* conception and the *inherent rights* conception. I noted that right order theorists can in principle join with inherent rights theorists in holding that there are natural rights—though most do not; the essential difference between the two conceptions lies not there but in how the deep structure of the moral order is understood.

The inherent rights theorist holds that there is something about persons and human beings that, all by itself, gives them certain rights; there doesn't have to be anything outside them that somehow confers those rights on them. The theory of claim-rights that I have articulated is an inherent rights theory; I hold that it is on account of our worth, our dignity, that we have rights.

The right order theorist holds, on the contrary, that having dignity is not enough to give someone rights, nor is there anything else about persons or human beings that is sufficient. Always there has to be an external standard of some sort that directly or indirectly bestows rights on them. Absent that external standard and its application to specific cases, nobody has any natural rights.

We have seen that Scripture presupposes the existence of natural rights, both divine and human. Does it also presuppose one or another of these two ways of thinking about justice and rights, the inherent rights way or the right order way?

On first blush, the prominence in Scripture of divine commandments would seem to indicate that the biblical writers presupposed the right order conception; the content of the divine commandments would be the objective standard that indirectly bestows or confers rights. That's how Joan Lockwood O'Donovan understands what she calls "the objective matrix of obligations"; the objective matrix is the content of God's commands. God issues commandments to us. Those commandments generate in us the obligation toward God to obey God by doing what God commands; and that obligation has, as its correlative, God's claim-right against us that we obey God by doing what God commands.

For example, God enjoins us not to murder. That generates in each of us the obligation toward God to obey God by not murdering anyone; God then has the correlative claim-right against each of us that we obey God by not murdering our fellows. In the third commandment God enjoins us not to take the name of God in vain. That generates in each of us the obligation toward God to obey God by not taking God's name in vain; God then has the correlative claim-right against each of us that we obey God by not taking God's name in vain.

But rather than going with surface appearance, let's think a bit more deeply about the matter. If one is not permitted to command someone to do something, then going ahead and doing so does not generate in one's addressee the obligation to do what one commanded. If one soldier orders another to do something without being permitted to do so—without having the authority to do so—then ordering the fellow soldier to do it does not place the fellow soldier under obligation to do what was commanded. To say the same thing a bit differently: only if one is permitted to command someone to do a certain thing does one's command generate in the addressee the obligation to do it.

How do we come to have such permissions—call them, *command-permissions*? Often they are bestowed on us by some action performed by some person or group of persons. Specifically, the bestowal often comes along with being appointed to some office or position. A military person is appointed captain. Among the things that she is now permitted (authorized) to do is issue commands of certain sorts to the troops under her command. When she does in fact issue a command of that sort to them, she generates in those to whom she issues the command the obligation to obey her by doing what she commanded; she then has the correlative right to their obeying her by doing what she commanded.

It seems clear, however, that not all command-permissions are in this way bestowed on us. I take it that parents are permitted to command their children to do or refrain from doing certain things. But nobody bestowed that permission on them. The bestowal did not come along with their appointment to the office of parent; the natural parents of a child were never appointed to the office of parent. There's just something about being parents that gives parents the authority (permission) to issue commands to their children. So far as I can see, it is on account of their being the procreators of the child that they have this particular permission-right. It's a *natural* permission-right.

Let's apply these lessons to God. The commands God issues to us generate in us the obligation toward God to obey God by doing what God commanded; and those obligations have, as their correlatives, God's claim-right against us to our obeying God by doing what God commanded. They generate those obligations in us because God is *permitted* to issue to us these commands; God has the permission-right to do so, the authority to do so.

And what is it that accounts for God's having these command-permissions? Were they somehow bestowed on God? Do they come along with some office to which God has been appointed?

They were certainly not bestowed on God by us; there is no office to which we have appointed God. The very idea is ludicrous. Were they bestowed on God by himself? Did God appoint himself to some office, and did certain command-permissions just automatically come along with appointment to that office? The idea makes no sense.

Rather than thinking of God's command-permissions on analogy to those of some captain, we should think of them on analogy to the command-permissions of parents.

A fundamental presupposition of the biblical writers is that God has the authority (permission) to issue commands to human beings by virtue of being their creator. And God has the authority (permission) to issue commands to Israel, in particular, by virtue of having delivered Israel from slave bondage. Surely that is the import of the anguished divine cry that I quoted earlier from the prophet Micah. Let me quote it again:

> The LORD has a controversy with his people,
>   and he will contend with Israel.
> "O my people, what have I done to you?
>   in what have I wearied you? Answer me!
> For I brought you up from the land of Egypt,
>   and redeemed you from the house of bondage."
>   (Mic. 6:2–4)

In the moral framework expressed and presupposed by the biblical writers, God has the authority (permission-right) to issue commands to us; that's why the commands generate obligations in us and correlative rights in God. But God does not have that right because we have bestowed it on him; nor does God have it because God bestowed in on himself. God has it on account of being our creator and redeemer. God's right to issue commands to us is an *inherent* right.

Let me close this chapter with a comment about my explanation of the inherent rights way of thinking. I said that the inherent rights theorist holds that there is something about persons and human beings that, all by itself, gives them certain rights; some of their rights are such that there isn't anything outside them that somehow bestows or confers those rights on them. In offering this explanation of the inherent rights way of thinking, I did not distinguish claim-rights from permission-rights. I meant the explanation to apply to both sorts of rights.

The theory of inherent rights that I have worked out is a theory of claim-rights; I have not developed a theory of permission-rights. Were I to develop a theory of permission-rights, it too would be an inherent rights theory. For what we have just now seen is that at least some of the permission-rights that persons and human beings possess are not bestowed but inherent.

PART 4

RIGHTING INJUSTICE

❖ 20 ❖

Human Rights

I have said nothing so far about human rights. It's time that I did. People often confuse human rights with the rights that human beings have. It's easy to see why they do; animal rights, after all, are the rights that animals have. But as the term "human rights" has come to be used, human rights are just a species of the rights that human beings have. Recall my example of the student who did top-notch work in a course I was teaching. He has a right to an A on his record; but that right is not a human right.

In my book *Justice: Rights and Wrongs*, I postponed my discussion of human rights until near the end. I did so in order to convey the idea that rights are vastly more extensive than human rights. And I wanted my theory of rights to be a theory of claim-rights in general, not just of those that are human rights. I seem to have failed; a good number of intelligent readers have taken my account of human rights to be my theory of rights in general.

So what are *human* rights? The twentieth century was a century of great moral horror; it was also a century of great moral achievement, the achievement being in good measure a response to the horror. In speaking of great moral achievement, I have in mind the various

United Nations (UN) declarations on human rights, plus the gradual embodiment of human rights into national and international law and jurisprudence.

The UN documents do not explain what a human right is; after a few introductory comments, they each just give a list of rights. But the writers, in deciding what to put on the list, would have employed some understanding of what a human right is. So one way of getting hold of the concept of a human right would be to take the lists of human rights that we find in the UN documents and try to surmise the concept implicit in those lists. Another way of getting hold of the concept would be to look at the explanation of the concept given by philosophers, political theorists, and legal theorists.

Contrary to what one might expect, these two approaches yield very different results. The common explanation of a human right is that it is a right that one has just by virtue of being a human being. Or to put the same point in slightly different terminology: a human right is a right such that the status sufficient for possessing the right is that of being a human being. One doesn't have to be a *Greek* human being, a *male* human being, an *educated* human being. One doesn't have to be any particular kind of human being whatsoever, not even a human being capable of functioning as a *person*. It's enough that one has the status of being a human being.

Ambrose, Basil, and John Chrysostom assumed that just by virtue of being a human being one has a right to something like fair and reasonable access to adequate means of sustenance. That right is, then, a human right. John explicitly makes the point that one doesn't have to be a virtuous human being to have this right; it's sufficient that one be a human being.

The UN lists of human rights confront us with items that do not fit this explanation. To take just one example: article 23 of the Universal Declaration of Human Rights says that "everyone has the right to work, to free choice of employment, to just and favourable conditions of work, and to protection against unemployment." To have this right it's not enough that one be a human being; one has to be a particular *kind* of human being—namely, a human being capable of working. Not all human beings are capable of working: infants are not, those sunk into advanced dementia are not.

The explanation of why these two approaches yield different results seems to me to be that those who composed the UN documents did not have in mind all human beings whatsoever. They did not have in mind infants, those in a permanent coma, or those in advanced dementia. The rights they cite are, for the most part, the rights of normal adults or children in typical situations in the modern world. It is these particular human beings that the writers of the UN documents seem to have had their eye on.

So we have to make a choice. Shall we be guided in our understanding of what a human right is by the standard explanation, and accordingly understand a human right as a right that one has just by virtue of being a human being, or shall we instead be guided by the concept implicit in the common lists of human rights? I propose that we do the former.[1]

For rights in general, and so also for human rights, it's important to distinguish between the rights that one has *other things being equal*, and the rights that one has *all things considered*. The point, of course, is that other things may not be equal. Sometimes honoring one person's "other-things-being-equal" rights conflicts with honoring those of one or more others. Then one has to make an "all-things-considered" judgment as to which of those rights is the weightier. If one makes the correct judgment and acts thereon, one will deprive someone of her "other-things-being-equal" rights, but not of her "all-things-considered" rights. In doing so, one will not have wronged her; one will not have treated her with less than due respect for her worth. One wrongs someone only if one violates her "all-things-considered" rights.

---

1. I discuss the sort of rights that the UN documents list—I call them *human person rights*—in my essay "Grounding the Rights We Have as Human Persons." The essay is included in my *Understanding Liberal Democracy* (Oxford: Oxford University Press, 2012).

What I have been calling "other-things-being-equal" rights are typically called *prima facie* rights by philosophers; what I have been calling "all-things-considered" rights are typically called *ultima facie* rights. Let me henceforth use this terminology.

Given the trumping force of rights, a *prima facie* right can be outweighed only by other *prima facie* rights, not by mere goods to which no one has a *prima facie* right. It may be that certain *prima facie* human rights are never outweighed by any other *prima facie* rights. I judge that one's right not to be tortured for the pleasure of the torturer is an example of such.

It's also worth noting that one's right to be treated a certain way may be a human right even though one finds oneself in a circumstance where one does not have the right—that is to say, in a circumstance where it is not even among one's *prima facie* rights. This would be the case if one found oneself in a circumstance where it was impossible to be rendered the good to which one has the right. Suppose that Ambrose, Basil, and John were right, that among our human rights is the right to fair and reasonable access to adequate means of sustenance. The status sufficient for having the right is that of being a human being, not any particular sort of human being, just a human being. But should one's circumstance be that of extreme widespread drought with no means of sustenance available to anyone, one would, in that circumstance, not have that right. One would not be wronged in being deprived of means of sustenance. It's true of rights in general that one does not have a right to be treated a certain way if it's impossible that one be treated that way.[2]

Once we have identified those rights of human beings that are human rights, the most important question confronting us is, what accounts for our having these rights? What grounds them?

2. The distinction between *status* and *circumstance* that I employed in the text above is crucial for understanding rights in general, but especially human rights. A right that one has is a human right if the only *status* one needs to possess the right is that of being human; but there may be *circumstances* in which one does not possess the right, not even as a *prima facie* right, because in those circumstances one cannot be treated in accord with the right.

It should be noted that one may firmly believe that there are human rights without being able to ground or account for them. That is, in fact, the situation of most people who work for human rights or write about them; most of them cannot articulate a successful grounding.

There is nothing irrational about being in such a situation. The perennial situation of philosophers and other theorists is that they firmly believe that such-and-such is the case, but find themselves incapable at the time of accounting for it—they believe, for example, that there is such a thing as moral obligation but find themselves incapable of giving a satisfactory account of it. An account would be a good thing to have; it would be desirable to have an account. If no satisfying theoretical account is forthcoming, one might eventually begin to doubt the existence of the phenomenon. But being unable to account for something that one believes to be the case does not imply that one should give up believing that there is such a thing. And it certainly does not imply that there is no such thing.

The UN declarations are all dignity-based documents. They all affirm or assume that human rights accrue to human beings on account of the dignity that human beings possess—their worth, their excellence, their estimability. Given my account of rights in general, I think this is correct.

Worth, dignity, excellence does not just settle on things willy-nilly; always there's something about the thing that gives it worth, something that accounts for its worth, something on which its worth supervenes. If the painting that you just finished is a fine painting, then there's something about it that makes it fine. We may find it difficult if not impossible to put that into words; but it makes no sense to say that it's a fine painting but that there's nothing about it that makes it fine. So what is it about human beings that gives them the dignity that grounds their human rights?

A feature of the UN documents that has often been noted is that, though they affirm or assume that all human beings have dignity and that their human rights are grounded in that dignity, they refrain from making any attempt to account for that dignity. They make no attempt to specify that feature of human beings on which the relevant dignity supervenes. From various narratives concerning the origin of these documents, we know the reason for this silence. Those who composed the original UN declaration discussed the basis of human dignity but found themselves disagreeing on the matter; so they decided to remain silent.

Almost all secular proposals concerning the ground of human rights are dignity-based accounts; and almost all of those, in turn, are what one might call *capacity accounts*; they hold that the worth that grounds human rights supervenes on a certain capacity that human beings have.

There is remarkable unanimity on the capacity proposed. To the best of my knowledge, it is always either the capacity for rational agency in general, or some specific form of that capacity, such as the capacity for acting out of duty, the capacity for acting on an apprehension of the good, or the capacity for forming, implementing, and revising a plan of life. The basic idea goes back to Immanuel Kant.

The capacity for rational agency is a remarkable capacity; it gives those who possess it great worth. The problem, however, for those who want to ground human rights in the worth we have by virtue of possessing this capacity is that some human beings do not have the capacity: newborn infants do not yet have the capacity, those sunk deep into dementia or in a permanent coma no longer have it, those severely impaired mentally from birth never have it. Yet they have rights—the right, for example, not to be shot and have their bodies tossed into a dumpster for waste management to haul away.

In chapter 15 of *Justice: Rights and Wrongs*, I explored various attempts to revise the straightforward capacities account so that the revised account avoids this problem. I argued there that all the revisions fail. Each of them has one or another unacceptable implication; and all together they fail in such ways that one can see that, in general, capacity accounts will not work. Rather than repeating here what I said there, I refer the reader to my book.[3]

---

3. *Justice: Rights and Wrongs* (Princeton: Princeton University Press, 2008). A later and improved presentation of the argument is to be found in my essay "On Secular and

So why do we—some of us, anyway—ascribe dignity even to those human beings so severely impaired as never to have the capacity for rational agency or any other capacity that might be thought to give them dignity? Let me offer a suggestion that seems to me worth considering.

Notice that no matter how severely impaired a human being may be, she retains human nature; indeed, to say that she is impaired is to presuppose that she has a nature, a nature that is impaired in its functioning.

Human nature is truly noble. No nonhuman animal has so remarkable a nature. So may it be that what gives even the most impaired human beings the dignity that grounds human rights is that they possess human nature? May it be that their possession of human nature is what gives them the relevant dignity?

How can we wrap our minds around this proposal? Let me make a suggestion. Think of our human nature as our design-plan, and then consider what we would say about other cases of well-formed and malformed exemplifications of a design-plan. Suppose that my two neighbors own examples of the same model of automobile, a certain model of Jaguar, let's say. The example that my neighbor to the east owns is well formed in all respects, and I admire it enormously. The example that my neighbor to the west owns has been in a wreck; the mechanics and body repair shops all tell him that repairing it would require such extensive replacement of parts that it's best to scrap it.

Would I advise my neighbor to the west to reject this advice and instead treasure his automobile as something of great worth on account of its design-plan? Would I advise him to store it in his garage under a dust cover, every now and then lifting up the cover to admire the remains? Would I tell him that the mechanics and body repair shops, in advising him to scrap it, were ignoring the fact that his automobile is an example of the very same model whose well-formed example is so admirable?

Theistic Groundings of Human Rights." The essay is included in my *Understanding Liberal Democracy* (Oxford: Oxford University Press, 2012).

I would not. I would advise him to sell it for scrap. It has no other worth than its worth as scrap metal, plastic, leather, and glass.

Perhaps some readers will disagree with this judgment; perhaps some would advise him to keep it on the ground that its noble design-plan gives it great worth. By analogy, they would say that the human nature that each and every human being possesses gives him or her the dignity that grounds their human rights. Anyone who holds this view thereby has a secular grounding of human rights.

Almost all Christians who have thought and written about human rights hold that our bearing the image of God is what gives us the dignity that grounds human rights. To decide whether this suggestion is tenable, we have to know what constitutes the image of God.

The history of Christian (and Jewish) thought contains a quite astounding diversity of proposals. To the best of my knowledge, however, all of them are of one or the other of two sorts. Some writers understand the image of God as consisting of resembling God with respect to certain capacities. Others understand it as consisting of resembling God, or representing God, with respect to a certain role in creation—the role of "having dominion," for example. Any such role obviously requires the possession of certain capacities.

The main point made above about secular capacity accounts applies here as well: whatever be the capacities required to possess the image of God, some human beings do not have those capacities. If the image of God is understood in the traditional way, as presupposing or consisting of the possession of certain capacities, then some human beings lack the image of God.

The alternative secular grounding that I set forth for consideration suggests an alternative way of understanding the image of God. Rather than understanding the image as consisting of resembling God with respect to certain capacities, or as resembling or representing God with respect to a certain role in creation, we could understand it as consisting of having a nature that resembles God. As we noted earlier, no matter how impaired a human being may be, she nonetheless possesses human nature. In possessing such a nature, she resembles God in a certain way. One might call this a *nature-resemblance* account of the image of God, in place of the traditional *capacities-resemblance* or *role-resemblance* accounts.

I expressed my doubts about the proposal that human rights are grounded in human nature. What the theistic account we are presently considering adds to the secular account is that we resemble God with respect to our nature. I find this theistic adaptation of the nature account no more convincing than the original. Suppose someone points out to me that the design-plan of the wrecked automobile of my neighbor to the west is not only identical with the design-plan of my other neighbor's automobile, but rather similar to the design-plan of a yet more noble automobile. Would that be a reason for me to change my advice? It would not.

What does ground human rights in the Christian vision of things, so I suggest, is God's love for each and every one of God's human creatures—more specifically, God's desire for friendship or fellowship with each and every human being. An analogy may once again help in thinking about the idea.

Imagine a good monarch who bestows on all his subjects the great benefit of a just political order that serves the common good. But he's rather lonely. So in addition to acting as a benefactor to all his subjects, he decides to choose some as those with whom he would like to be friends. This is an honor for the ones chosen. "I am honored that you would choose me to be your friend," they say. No doubt over the course of time various goods in their lives will ensue from the monarch's being friends with them. But just to be chosen as one with whom the monarch would like to be a friend is an honor. Those chosen will cite that fact under "Honors" in their *curricula vitae*. Those not chosen will be envious.

Here's the crucial point. To be honored is to have worth bestowed on one. Admittedly this is somewhat mysterious. But an indication of the fact that this is what happens is that to be honored is to acquire a new ground for respect, and hence new ways in which one can be demeaned and wronged; and that's possible only if there has been some alteration in one's worth. The most obvious way in which one can now be demeaned and wronged is by having the honor itself belittled. One who has not been chosen by the monarch for friendship sarcastically remarks to someone who has been chosen, "Big deal!" The latter has a right to be angry; this is a snub.

The application of the analogy is obvious. Suppose that one is a creature chosen by God as someone with whom God desires to be a friend. This is to be honored by God. And to be honored by God is to have worth bestowed on one. Add now that every human being has the honor of being chosen by God as someone with whom God desires to be a friend, and that this desire endures. Then every human being has the equal and ineradicable worth that being so honored bestows on him or her.

A question to consider is whether, on this view of things, it is purely whimsical and arbitrary of God to choose human beings as the creatures with whom God wants to be friends. Might God just as well have chosen crocodiles? No. Though the monarch may well not look for the most estimable people in the realm when settling on those with whom he would like to be friends, he does look for those in whom he sees potential for friendship. Crocodiles lack the potential for being friends with God. To be a friend with God requires that one have the nature of a person. Crocodiles at their best cannot be persons. Of all the animals, it's only human animals that can function as persons and can thus be friends with God.

The same consideration that makes it understandable why God did not choose crocodiles for friendship makes it understandable why God chose human beings. Since it's in our nature to be persons, we have the potential for friendship with God. Of course there are blockages to the realization of that potential that have to be overcome by God and us. The moral breach between us of our having wronged God will have to be repaired; and those who cannot presently function as persons will have to be healed, in this life or the next, of that deep malformation. Though God's desire for friendship with some human being does not presuppose that that human being presently has the capacities necessary for the satisfaction of that desire, it does presuppose that that human being *will some day* have those capacities, in this life or the next.

The grounding of human rights that I have just articulated is a grounding that could be affirmed by Jews and Muslims as well as Christians. Let me conclude by suggesting an additional grounding that is distinctly Christian. I will be brief.

Christians hold that, in Jesus, the Second Person of the Trinity assumed our human nature. This is an extraordinary honor for human beings. To each of us the Second Person of the Trinity pays the honor of assuming our nature, thereby sharing our nature with us. We each have no greater dignity than that. To torture a human being is to torture a creature whose nature he or she shares with the Second Person of the Trinity.

❖ 21 ❖

Six Days in South Africa

I developed a theory of primary justice, I argued for the importance of justice so understood, and I explored the relation between love and justice. Alongside these philosophical reflections I lent my support to the cause of the people of color in South Africa and to the cause of the Palestinians. Mainly this support consisted of giving talks and writing articles in which I tried to awaken my listeners and readers to the injustice of what was going on. On one occasion, in 1985, it involved direct participation in the struggle to right injustice in South Africa. The experience gave me a glimpse of some fascinating features of the struggle as it was then taking place. I described the experience afterward in an article that I published.[1] Here is part of what I wrote.

The call from Allan Boesak came early on the morning of Tuesday, October 15: would I come to Cape Town as soon as possible to testify on his behalf in the hearing to get his bail conditions lifted?

1. "Six Days in South Africa," *The Reformed Journal* 35, no. 12 (December 1985): 15–21.

I had come to know Allan in the academic year 1980–81 when he was the first Multi-Cultural Lecturer at Calvin College. My wife, Claire, and I became close friends with Allan. To the call for help from a brother one does not say no. But could I really be of help—I, a philosophy professor from a college in midwestern America?

Saturday night I was on the plane in New York, visa in hand, and on Sunday night I stepped out to be greeted by Allan, his family, and a friend. We had to cut short our catching up around their kitchen table in the Cape Town suburb of Bellville because the next day Allan had to go early into downtown Cape Town to prepare the case with his attorneys.

As we were driving into the city the next morning, I saw a strange khaki-colored vehicle on the road in front of us, rather like a bus, but open at the top, so that if people stood up in it their heads would poke out. The glass at the sides was obviously bulletproof, and everything else was plated with armor. "What's that?" I asked. "A casspir," said Allan. I did not ask what casspirs were for.

During my stay I saw a casspir in action only on videotape. Police were standing up in the casspir, pointing guns at school children, while other police were standing on the ground firing tear gas canisters into the school. The police force was integrated—mostly white, but some "blacks." The school was not integrated: only "black" children came pouring out, sneezing, coughing, crying hysterically, tumbling over the fence, fear and hate mingled on their faces. Apparently their crime was that they had been active in protest rallies the previous day.

For twenty-six days during September, Allan had been held in solitary confinement. With one exception, the only person he saw during that time was his interrogator, Major Nel. His wife was allowed to see him once, for one hour, with Major Nel standing by watching and listening. She was not allowed to talk about happenings in South Africa and the world, only about their family. His captors allowed Allan no book other than his Bible, and they allowed him no paper.

Upon releasing him from jail the government filed charges against him—though even now the bill of charges is not final. The charge, currently, is that of sedition, as specified in the security legislation. The acts Boesak is alleged to have committed, and which the government contends are acts of sedition, are recommending a consumers' boycott, recommending a school boycott, recommending disinvestment, and helping to plan an illegal march on Pollsmoor Prison. Allan denied that he ever recommended a school boycott. He freely admits having done the other things—though whether these are acts of sedition as defined in the security legislation is a matter that has not yet been tested in court.

The bail conditions on which Boesak was released included such normal conditions as the payment of 20,000 Rand, the stipulation that he not communicate with state witnesses, and the stipulation that while out on bail he not commit acts of the sort for which he was charged. But the other conditions had the effect of placing him under house arrest; they made it impossible for him to do the work to which he has been called. The hearing was to ask the court to order the government to lift the "house arrest" conditions. Boesak's attorney would argue that if the government wanted to ban him, they had to do so straightforwardly and live with the consequences. What they could not do is ban him under the guise of setting bail conditions.

The bail conditions Boesak was protesting were that he sign in at the Bellville police station every day before 9:00 a.m.; that he be in his house every night between 9:00 p.m. and 6:00 a.m.; that he not leave his suburb of Bellville without the written permission of the police; that he surrender his passport; that he attend no meeting of more than ten people, except for regular services at his own church, without written permission of the police; that he not visit any educational institution except to pay calls on student members of his congregation; that he not submit to any media interviews; and that he not attend any funerals except with police permission.

To prevent crowds, the case had been moved from Cape Town to the small village of Malmesbury about forty-five minutes away. We learned that the proceedings would begin on Wednesday and then resume on Friday. I would be the first witness, since I could not stay into the next week and the attorney was unable to predict whether the hearing would take more than two days.

What was it that Boesak and his attorney wanted from me? To testify that it was indeed indispensable for Boesak to have his passport back if he was to do the work that the Reformed churches of the world had asked him to do in appointing him head of the World Alliance of Reformed Churches. Second, to testify that Boesak, of all people, would not flee the country and fail to stand trial. If it became relevant, to testify, third, that I had always known him to recommend nonviolent resistance. And finally, if the government contended that ministers of the gospel, such as Boesak, should stick to purely "spiritual" matters and stay out of politics, to testify that an important strand in the Reformed tradition has always been to refuse to accept any dichotomy between the "spiritual" and the political. After a long day of preparation, we returned to the Boesak home in Bellville—which now in daylight I could see to be a simple, somewhat dull suburb reserved for "colored" people.

The next morning I was introduced to a daily routine. About 7:15 a call came informing Allan about the people who had been taken into detention the night before—many of them friends and acquaintances of his. For the rest of the week the same call would come each morning a bit after 7:00. On Friday morning the caller reported that more than eighty people in the Cape area had been arrested the previous night, including the entire executive board of the United Democratic Front, university professors, and student leaders. One of those detained was Charles Villa-Vicenzio, theologian from the University of Cape Town. Charles is an acquaintance of mine who had been scheduled to come over to the Boesak home that evening.

Wednesday morning we drove out to Malmesbury. Malmesbury, I would judge, is a village of some twenty-five hundred people. Police were everywhere in the center of the village. I asked someone how many he thought there were. Maybe two hundred, he said. I had not seen such a concentration of firepower since early 1982 in Beirut. These police were older and more professional looking than the militia in Beirut, however. The courtroom held about sixty people, kept in order by the police. Almost everybody in the audience was a person of color. The main language of the hearing was English, but when a witness felt more comfortable with Afrikaans, the language shifted over to that for the witness's testimony.

In South African law there are three standard considerations for setting bail. The state wants to be assured that the accused will stand trial, that the accused will not interfere with state witnesses, and that while out on bail the accused will not again commit the acts with which he or she is charged. The state had stipulated in its bail conditions that Boesak not do either of the latter two; these stipulations he was not contesting. Hence the only issue left—so it seemed—was whether he would likely flee the country if his "house arrest" were lifted.

I stepped into the witness box and was sworn in. I testified that if ever anyone deserved to be released on his recognizance, it was Boesak. All he stood for, and all that he had been struggling for, would come crashing down if he did not stand trial. And I testified that Boesak had to be present on the international scene if he was to do the work that the worldwide church had asked him to do.

In his cross-examination of me, the state attorney did not question my testimony that Boesak would definitely stand trial. Nor did he question my testimony that Boesak was needed on the international scene. Thus it would seem that the "house arrest" conditions should be lifted. What purpose in law did they serve other than assuring the state that Boesak would be available for trial? Instead, the state attorney pressed me on Boesak's commitment to nonviolence. I testified, as firmly as I knew how, that he was indeed committed to nonviolent protest.

"You know, do you not, that there is a good deal of unrest and violence in South Africa at present?"

"Yes, I have read about that."

"And you are aware that a good deal of this unrest and violence has followed speeches by Boesak?"

"About that I do not know. But I did read that violence followed the speech of the state president in August. Yet your government did not regard that as a reason for silencing the state president."

"No further questions."

To Boesak's attorney (though not to me) the strategy of the state was now clear. South African law contains a provision that says that beyond the standard considerations, bail conditions may also be set by reference to state security. It appears that considerations of state security have never in fact been decisive in setting bail. What the state would argue was that in this case, for the first time, state security should be the decisive consideration. But how exactly did they think that Boesak endangered the security of the state of South Africa? That would become clear in due course.

Boesak himself was to be the next witness; but before he took the stand, a recess was declared. Most of us went out into the court-yard—we few whites amidst the "blacks" and "coloreds," all sur-rounded by white policemen. There was a great deal of laughter and joking. I recalled what I had also noticed in the Middle East: the oppressors are grim while the oppressed laugh and tell jokes. The policemen keeping their eye on us were grim. Even grimmer was Major Nel, who was to testify against Boesak for the state on Friday. He had found a chair in the courtroom separated from the rest of us; there he remained sitting in catatonic sobriety, legs crossed, staring fixedly across the room.

Recess over, Boesak was put in the witness box. In cross-examining him the state attorney, quite incredibly, gave him wide-open opportu-nities to make eloquent speeches, never cutting him off.

"How can we be assured that if your passport is returned, you will not leave the country and not stand trial?"

"I would never abandon my people. To the contrary, I would relish standing trial to speak the truth about this country."

"Is it not true that you think it appropriate to engage in political activities in addition to your work as minister?"

"I do not regard my political activities as something in addition to my call as minister of the gospel. I come from a tradition, the Reformed tradition, in which we refuse to separate the political from the spiritual. As Abraham Kuyper said, there is not one square inch of this world that does not belong to the Lordship of Jesus Christ." (Allan says that here he saw a smile cross the face of the magistrate; later we learned that he is an elder in the Dutch Reformed Church.)

"But is it not true that you have condoned violence?"

"I have consistently preached against violence. I have said that violence destroys the soul of those who commit violence. It is destroying the soul of the Afrikaner. Do you think I want it to destroy the soul of my own people as well? Besides, I have always said to the young people, 'You throw stones, they shoot bullets.'"

"But do you not agree that your speeches are very emotional and that they may well provoke violence whether you intend that or not?"

"Show me a single case in which that has been true."

"We shall produce evidence on Friday."

The court adjourned for lunch. We emerged from the courthouse to a crowd of a thousand people, mostly "black," neatly lined up along the street. They let forth a mighty cheer when they saw Boesak; when he walked across the street to shake hands with some, they broke their policed ranks and swirled around. For lunch we drove out of the white village to a restaurant in the adjoining black township. After perhaps half an hour inside, we came out to find ourselves again in the midst of a cheering crowd, this time of about twelve hundred students chanting, "Boesak, Boesak, Boesak," each one trying to shake Allan's hand.

Friday it was the state's opportunity to present its case. Major Nel was one of the two witnesses, the other being Captain van Schalkwijk, head of the riot police in Bellville. The strategy was now clear: to argue that Boesak's speeches provoked violence, that this violence endangered state security, and that for this reason his bail conditions should remain as they were. The state cited some four or five episodes that it regarded as decisive evidence that Boesak's speeches produced violence. The cross-examination of the witnesses by Boesak's attorney, Henrik Viljoen, was elegant.

It was alleged that Boesak had spoken at the University of the Western Cape on July 25 and that, as the result of his speech, the students had rioted on July 26.

Viljoen: "Major Nel, are you quite certain that the speech occurred on July 25?"

Nel: "Yes I am."

"And that the riot occurred on the 26th?"

"Yes."

"And that it was Dr. Boesak who spoke on that night?"

"That is correct."

"No one else?"

"No, just Dr. Boesak."

"And that he spoke at the University of the Western Cape?"

"Yes."

"And that the riot occurred at the same university?"

"Yes."

"The next day?"

"Yes."

"Well, I do not wish to embarrass you, Major Nel. But Dr. Boesak could not have spoken at the University of the Western Cape on July 25. He was in the United States on that day. He has plane tickets to prove it."

"Then my information must be mistaken."

What was happening? I asked myself. Whatever else was to be said about the Afrikaners, I had always thought that they were competent. But this was astounding incompetence.

Another key episode in the state's case was a riot of the students at the University of the Western Cape on July 29. Van Schalkwijk had a photo of Boesak among the uproarious students.

Viljoen: "Did you hear what Boesak said to the students?"

Van Schalkwijk: "No, I did not."

"So you do not directly know that he was stirring them up to violence?"

"No."

"Might he instead have been trying to calm them down?"

"That is possible."

At this point Viljoen presented as witness an official from the university who testified that, on the day in question, a riot was already taking place at the university when the rector called Boesak at his home and asked him to come to the university as soon as possible to calm the students.

So it went, for all the other alleged episodes of Boesak's speeches provoking violence. What we were seeing, I concluded, was the incompetence that flows from the arrogance of power. When political clout wins all your cases, competence is a dispensable commodity.

Apparently chastened by the repeated, "Then my information must be mistaken" of his witnesses, the state attorney in his closing argument never tried to connect Boesak to violence. He just said that South Africa was experiencing a great deal of unrest and that there was ample ground in the law for setting bail by reference to state security. No doubt he was hoping that the magistrate would draw connections that his own argument did not. Viljoen was eloquent in showing that the state's case was entirely void of merit. We emerged from the courthouse into a yet larger crowd of yet more loudly cheering supporters than on the Wednesday before.

The hearing had gone in Boesak's favor beyond anything we had dared hope. On the evidence, and on the law, the magistrate could not decide anything other than to lift all the contested provisions. Insofar as one could read his face, he was sympathetic. Yet we were apprehensive. Magistrates, after all, are human beings with a natural desire to please their superiors. What we expected was a compromise that, while giving Allan some of what he asked for, would not seriously embarrass the state.

The Boesak house that late afternoon was filled with laughter and excited talk. After a late supper we watched a videotape of one of the United Democratic Front rallies at which Allan had spoken. Clearly these rallies were not only very moving occasions but also great fun, with singing, chanting, and rhyming. Here is part of one of the rhymes:

> Die oumas, die oupas,
> die mammas, die pappas,
> die boeties, die sussies,
> die hondjies, die katjies,
> is saam in die struggle.

> The grandmas, the grandpas,
> the mamas, the papas,
> the brothers, the sisters,
> the dogs, the cats,
> are together in the struggle.

Each time Allan would shout out the first words of a line—for example, "die oumas"—the crowd in rhythm would shout out the next words—"die oupas." They also interspersed the lines with the Xhosa sentence, *Amandla ngawethu*—"the power is ours." The effect was hypnotic.

Saturday the Boesaks drove me to the airport. After a warm farewell at the ticket counter I walked straight ahead to the passport checker. "Was that Dr. Boesak you were with there?" he asked. "Yes, I replied." He wrote something down. "I see from this that you stayed at 6 Hoekstraat in Bellville; isn't that Dr. Boesak's address?" "Yes," I said. He wrote again, more lengthily this time. Then he sent me on my way with the hope that I would have a good trip back.

Monday a week later the magistrate was to deliver his opinion. Around 6:00 p.m. Cape Town time I called to find out the news. The background noise in the Boesak house told me. The magistrate had ordered all the contested provisions lifted, with the exception of the 20,000 Rand payment, and had gone out of his way to scold the state for the incompetence of its case. A man of courage and integrity! Allan added something ominous, however: "I think the government is going to play tricks with me and not give my passport back." Next day his suspicion was confirmed; the government refused to obey the magistrate's order to return the passport. Thus do those who loudly trumpet the supreme value of law and order disobey their own laws when that seems good in their eyes. They prize order—their order— more than law.

22

Art in the Struggle
to Right Injustice

During my six days in South Africa, there was much that I observed and learned about the struggle to right the injustice of apartheid that both fascinated and moved me. Though I did not myself observe or participate in a worship service during my stay, I learned of the central role of worship in the resistance movement; the anti-apartheid movement in South Africa resembled the civil rights movement in the United States in this respect. What I did observe firsthand was the role played by singing, chanting, storytelling, and the like.

I mentioned previously that one of my specialties within the field of philosophy was philosophy of art, or aesthetics, as it is often called. Philosophy of art of the past two and a half centuries has focused its attention almost exclusively on high art—those works of the arts that are displayed in museums and art galleries, performed in concert halls, or made available for reading in libraries. This is often said to be art "come into its own," in contrast to art which, so it is said, is in service to interests extraneous to art itself.

One of the major themes in modern philosophy of art is that of the separation of art from life. A well-known, rather over-the-top statement of the theme is the following passage from the 1913 publication *Art* by the English critic Clive Bell:

> To appreciate a work of art we need bring with us nothing from life, no knowledge of its ideas and affairs, no familiarity with its emotions. Art transports us from the world of man's activity to a world of aesthetic exaltation. For a moment we are shut off from human interests; our anticipations and memories are arrested; we are lifted above the stream of life. . . . The rapt philosopher, and he who contemplates a work of art, inhabit a world with an intense and peculiar significance of its own; that significance is unrelated to the significance of life.[1]

Bell confesses that sometimes he slips into

> using art as a means to the emotions of life and reading into it the ideas of life. I have been cutting blocks with a razor. I have tumbled from the superb peaks of aesthetic exaltation to the snug foothills of warm humanity. It is a jolly country. No one need be ashamed of enjoying himself there. Only no one who has ever been on the heights can help feeling a little crest-fallen in the cosy valleys. And let no one imagine, because he has made merry in the warm tilth and quaint nooks of romance, that he can even guess at the austere and thrilling raptures of whose who have climbed the cold, white peaks of art.[2]

Though I avoided such high-flown Romantic rhetoric, in my early years of teaching aesthetics I too focused my attention on high art and accepted the doctrine of the separation of art from life.

Then one Saturday afternoon I had an awakening in my living room in Grand Rapids, Michigan. I was listening to the University of Michigan radio station. Normally the station devoted Saturday afternoons to classical music. But the announcer said that today they were going to do something different; they were going to play work

1. Clive Bell, *Art* (New York: Putnam's Sons, 1958), 27–28.
2. Ibid., 31.

songs. For the first ten minutes or so I listened to these songs for their aesthetic qualities; I found them simple but fascinating.

Then cognitive dissonance welled up within me. These songs were not intended to be enjoyed in one's leisure but to be sung while working. Those who sang them while working were not lifted above ordinary life but engaged in the life of the workaday world. And as to the claim that these songs represented music not come into its own: these songs came into their own when they were sung while working, not when listened to aesthetically in one's living room. That's what they were meant for. Were they, then, perhaps an inferior form of music? Why so? Is the activity of singing while working inferior to the activity of listening aesthetically to some work of music? I saw no reason to think that it was. But if not, then why are songs that reward singing while working inferior to music that rewards aesthetic listening?

It was this awakening that slowly led to the line of thought that I worked out in my 1980 publication *Art in Action*, in which I called attention to the vast diversity of ways in which art plays a role in human action, in addition to works of the arts serving as objects of aesthetic contemplation. The storytelling, the singing, the rhyming, the chanting that I observed in the anti-apartheid protest movement were a live demonstration of the point. It reminded me of the extraordinary role played by the song "We Shall Overcome" in the US civil rights movement.

What do work songs do? What's the difference between singing while working on the railroad and just working on the railroad? What do singing, chanting, rhyming, and the like do when embedded in some social protest movement? What's the difference between all together singing "We Shall Overcome" while holding hands and swaying back and forth, and all together just saying the words? These are not easy questions to answer.

It appears to me that singing while working on the railroad is sometimes a way of expressing one's feelings about one's work; it sets one's work within an emotional context. Perhaps it also distracts somewhat from the tedium of the work; I would guess that those who reminisce about their work on the railroad say to each other, "Remember how we used to sing while we were working?" And perhaps singing while working sometimes serves to ennoble the work, to elevate it, to lend it some dignity.

Singing, chanting, and rhyming do similar things in protest movements—though as to distraction, my guess is that they distract less from tedium than from danger. But I think they do something else as well. They unite the members of the movement. Holding hands and swaying, we who joined in the civil rights movement sang, "We shall overcome, we shall overcome, we shall overcome some day, some day." Instead of singing, we could have simply said, "We shall overcome, we shall overcome." But the words without the music are flat, unremarkable; the music elevates the words. And saying them would not have had the mysterious uniting effect that singing them together had. So too, the people in the anti-apartheid movement were united in chanting responsively,

> Die oumas, die oupas,
> die mammas, die pappas,
> die boeties, die sussies,
> die hondjies, die katjies,
> is saam in die struggle.

Works of the arts also played another, quite different, role in the South African apartheid struggle. Among the books about South Africa that I bought over the years after my return from Potchefstroom were novels: Alan Paton's *Cry the Beloved Country* and *Too Late the Phalarope*, J. M. Coetzee's *The Life and Times of Michael K* and *Disgrace*, a number of novels by Nadine Gordimer, various writings by Breyten Breytenbach. On one visit to South Africa I attended a performance of one of Athol Fugard's plays.

All of these can be read in the Clive Bell way; we can lift them out of life and read them for their aesthetic qualities. But that is to read them with blinders on. These are about apartheid. Or better: they are not about that abstract thing, *apartheid*, but about human life *under* apartheid. Or better yet: they are not *about* life under apartheid; they *present* life under apartheid. They set life under apartheid before us. By doing so, they played a significant role in awakening the world to what life under apartheid was like.

In *Art in Action* I argued that we who are philosophers should attend to the many ways in which art is embodied in life and not focus our attention exclusively on high art. I did not take the next step of actually doing that. In particular, I did not discuss the role of art in social protest movements. I would like to do that some day. Among the "data" for my discussion would be what I observed about the role played by music, chant, fiction, and so forth in the South African anti-apartheid movement and in the US civil rights movement.

On the Blocking of Empathy and the Hardening of Hearts

I have often asked myself the question that I posed in my opening chapter: why did I respond so differently to the cry for justice by the so-called blacks and coloreds at the conference in Potchefstroom, and by the Palestinians on the west side of Chicago, than I did to the injustice of racial discrimination in my own country and to the injustice of the Vietnam War? The answer I have come up with is that in these conferences I was confronted with the faces and the voices of victims of systemic injustice. I fastened on their faces, absorbed their words, as they told their stories of daily humiliation, oppression, and demeaning. To generalize from my own experience: one of the most effective ways for those involved in social justice movements to energize support for their cause is to present to the public the faces and the voices of the wronged.

And what was it that seeing the faces and hearing the voices did to me? They evoked my empathy. By "empathy" I do not mean compassion; even less do I mean pity. I did feel compassion. But more than that: I found myself empathetically united with them, emotionally identified. I felt anger with their anger, humiliation with their humiliation, hurt with their hurt.

No doubt speeches and articles about the plight of the wronged sometimes evoke empathy. I think my own experience was more typical, however. I had read accounts of the situation in South Africa and in the Middle East. Those had not evoked empathy in me. It was seeing the faces and hearing the voices that evoked my empathy—*actual* faces and *actual* voices. Often film has the same effect; and sometimes prose fiction. The reason *Uncle Tom's Cabin* had such a powerful effect on the abolitionist movement in nineteenth-century America was that Harriet Beecher Stowe succeeded in putting the plight of the slave Tom so vividly before readers that many wept.

In whatever way the empathy is evoked, I think it is especially empathy with the wronged that energizes the struggle to right injustice. Some people are energized to support some struggle to right injustice by appeals to their sense of duty. Some may be energized by being persuaded that that's what the virtuous person does. Some may be energized by reading the prophetic literature of the Old Testament. The executive head of the Honduran organization Association for a More Just Society told me that he had recently been energized, even more than he was already, by sitting across the table from one of the men who was among the brains behind the assassination of one of the association's lawyers; he became intensely angry that this man was still free to perpetrate his foul deeds. But I think my case was typical: I was energized by my empathetic identification with those who told stories of their oppression and cried out for justice.

Sad to say, however, the faces and the voices of the wronged do not evoke empathy in all beholders and listeners. The faces and the voices that evoked empathy in me at the conference in Potchefstroom did not evoke empathy in the Afrikaners at the conference who spoke up in defense of apartheid. The faces and the voices of the Palestinians that evoked empathy in me did not evoke, and do not evoke, empathy in most Israelis and Americans. To use biblical language: their hearts are hardened. Why is that?

Sometimes hearts are hardened and empathy blocked because allowing the faces and the voices to evoke empathy would lead to acknowledging one's own complicity in the plight of the victims; that, in turn, would require reforming one's way of life, and that is more than one can bring oneself to do. One would be ostracized by friends, make less money, sacrifice one's position of privilege and power. Better to harden one's heart, hang on to one's social position, and every now and then make contributions to charitable organizations. That way, nothing has to change.

Another reason why hearts are often hardened and empathy blocked is that the hard-hearted have learned to dehumanize the victims—or if not precisely to dehumanize them, to think of them as lesser human beings with diminished sensibilities, sometimes even as loathsome. They are vermin, scum, Japs, dagos, Jew-boys. They are terrorists; nobody feels empathy for terrorists. An Israeli general was once quoted as calling the Palestinians "drugged cockroaches running around in a bottle." Arabs, it is said, respond only to force. Slave owners in the United States "embraced the fiction that black people lacked the capacity to feel deeply."[1] The slave traders of the nineteenth century thought of the human beings below deck as "cargo."[2] The Manhattanite who finds a homeless person sleeping on her doorstep when she steps out of her townhouse is revolted; she carefully steps over the person, being sure not to make bodily contact, and calls the police.

A third reason why hearts are often hardened and empathy blocked is that the hard-hearted have embraced a narrative that says that the plight of the victims is their own fault. The Palestinians, it is said, have refused to negotiate with Israel. Their misery is of their own making. Empathy is out of order. The poor are poor because they're lazy. Their poverty is of their own making. Empathy is inappropriate.

1. Heather Andrea Williams, *Help Me to Find My People* (Chapel Hill: University of North Carolina Press, 2012), quoted in Imani Perry, "Human Bonds," *The New York Times Sunday Book Review*, July 1, 2012, 11.
2. On this, see Adam Hochschild, *Bury the Chains* (Boston: Houghton Mifflin, 2005).

There is yet one more reason why hearts are often hardened and empathy blocked. The hard-hearted have embraced an ideology that says that some great good will be achieved by the present policies. Securing this great good comes at the cost of the suffering of some, and that's unfortunate. But the great good outweighs the suffering. To achieve the great good one must harden one's heart, stifle one's natural impulses to empathy, and do what the cause requires.[3]

In my reading I discovered that it was their embrace of an ideology of this visionary sort that blocked empathy on the part of Afrikaners and Israelis, combined, of course, with the other factors that I have mentioned. The Afrikaners were inspired, and the Israelis remain inspired, by the nineteenth-century Romantic ideology of nationalism, which held out the vision of each people achieving its own cultural and political identity and having its own state. The Afrikaners were struggling for their cultural identity and for a state of their own, an Afrikaner state; the Israelis have been struggling for their cultural identity and for a state of their own, a Jewish state. This is visionary politics.[4]

The problem with visionary nationalism is that, in the modern world, there are always persons of other nationalities mixed in with those who want a state of their own—persons of color mixed in with the Afrikaners, Palestinians mixed in with the Jews. These must either be expelled or reduced to second-class citizenship. For that to happen, those in power must harden their hearts. If they do not, their resolve will weaken and the visionary ideal will slip from their grasp.

Generalizing from my own experience, I have suggested that it is especially empathy for the plight of the victims of injustice that spurs us to support the struggle to right injustice. And I have suggested, again generalizing from my own experience, that it is especially seeing

3. In the film about the Khmer Rouge *Facing Genocide*, produced by the Swedish company Story Productions in 2010, Pol Pot is quoted as saying exactly this to his followers: to achieve the great task before them they must rid themselves of emotion and become purely rational.

4. In my *Until Justice and Peace Embrace* (Grand Rapids: Eerdmans, 1983) I discuss, in some detail, the role of visionary nationalism in South Africa and Israel.

the faces and hearing the voices of the victims of injustice that evokes empathy.

But empathy with the suffering may be evoked without exciting a passion for the righting of injustice. Not all suffering is the result of injustice; some is the result of natural causes. But even when suffering is the result of injustice, empathy sometimes evokes benevolent action to alleviate the plight of the victims rather than support for the struggle to right the injustice. We see photos of pitiful-looking orphans in Honduras. We respond empathetically. We do not ask whether these orphans are the victims of injustice. Out of the goodness of our hearts we send a contribution for the alleviation of their plight to the charitable organization whose name appears below the photo.

There are some complications here that call for unraveling. One is this: whether or not some particular person's suffering is the consequence of injustice, it may or may not be the case that justice requires that I come to her aid. Sometimes it does not; after all, nobody can come to the aid of everybody who needs aid. But sometimes justice does require action on our part. Sometimes I would wrong the person if I did not come to her aid. If justice does not require of me that I come to that person's aid, but I nonetheless do come to her aid, then my doing so is a case of gratuitous benevolence on my part; it's a case of justice-transcending benevolence.

Second, coming to the aid of someone who is the victim of injustice can take either or both of two forms. It can take the form of alleviating her suffering. Or it can take the form of supporting the struggle for the righting of the injustice.

Third, it's helpful to have in hand the distinction between what philosophers call *perfect* and *imperfect* duties, along with the corresponding distinction between *perfect* and *imperfect* rights. A *perfect duty* is the duty to treat a specific person in a specific way; an example would be my duty to give five dollars to the handicapped person sitting begging in front of my bank. An *imperfect duty* is the duty to treat someone or other in some specific way, but not any particular person, or to treat some specific person in some general way or other, but not in any particular way. My duty to give five dollars to one or another of the beggars on the mall, but not to any particular one, would be an imperfect duty, as would be my duty to give aid of some sort or other to the handicapped person sitting begging in front of my bank.

Here's another example of the distinction. On the one hand, I may have a duty to support the work of one or another social justice organization, such as the International Justice Mission or the Association for a More Just Society in Honduras, but not a duty to support any particular social justice organization. That would be an imperfect duty. On the other hand, because of my unique relationship to the Association for a More Just Society, I may have a duty to support *its* work. That would be a perfect duty. The same is true for supporting the work of relief organizations and development organizations. One may have an imperfect duty to support the work of one or another of these organizations, but not any particular one; or, because of the particularities of one's relation to one of them, one may have a perfect duty to support *its* work.

From these explanations of perfect and imperfect duties, it's easy to see what perfect and imperfect rights are. A *perfect* right is the right to be treated some specific way by some specific person—for example, the right of the handicapped person sitting begging in front of my bank to receive five dollars from me. An *imperfect* right, by contrast, is the right to be treated by someone or other in some specific way, or the right to be treated by some specific person in some way or other. The right of the handicapped person sitting begging in front of my bank to receive five dollars from someone or other, but not from any particular person, would be an example of an imperfect right, as would be that person's right to receive aid from me of some sort or other.

Fourth, it's helpful to distinguish between what I shall call *subjective* benevolence and what I shall call *objective* benevolence. Subjective benevolence consists of seeking to advance the well-being of someone without thinking of it as required by justice—either because one simply isn't thinking in terms of justice, or because one is thinking in those terms but sees oneself as going beyond what justice requires. Objective benevolence, then, consists of going beyond what justice *does in fact* require in seeking to advance someone's well-being. The person who acts out of subjective benevolence may or may not be performing an act of objective benevolence.

As I mentioned earlier, the Afrikaners present at the conference in Potchefstroom told stories about the charity that they extended to some of the so-called blacks and coloreds that they knew. I was not skeptical of those stories. I believed the stories they told about handing on clothes that their own children had outgrown to the children of the African family living in their backyard. And I did not doubt that, in many cases, this charity was evoked by empathy, or if not precisely by empathy, then by compassion. The Afrikaners at the conference did not strike me as hard-hearted. Later I would come across some who did.

Though the empathy of the Afrikaners at the conference was not blocked, it did not evoke in them support for the struggle to right injustice. Neither did it evoke in them recognition of the fact that they would wrong the family living in their backyard if they did not come to their aid. Instead it evoked subjective benevolence. Why was that? Why, in general, does empathy so often evoke subjective benevolence rather than recognition of the call to do justice and to support the struggle to right injustice?

Sometimes empathy does not evoke support for the struggle to right injustice because the empathetic person does not believe that the plight of those with whom he empathizes is in fact the result of injustice. Perhaps the thought never crosses his mind. Perhaps it crosses his mind but he is ignorant of the social analysis that brings to light the injustice of the situation. Or perhaps he knows about that analysis but believes that it is flawed. Whatever the cause, he is oblivious to the injustice. He only sees suffering people; he does not perceive the injustice that is the cause of their suffering. So of course he is not moved to support the struggle to right the injustice. The Afrikaners who spoke up in defense of apartheid at the conference did not accept that the so-called blacks and coloreds were being treated unjustly; they seemed honestly to believe that their plight was simply an unfortunate side effect of the struggle to achieve the great social good of apartheid. So of course their empathy did not move them to join in the struggle to right the injustice of apartheid.

But sometimes the reason is not oblivion but *resistance*—resistance to acknowledging that the plight of those who are suffering is the consequence of injustice, resistance also to acknowledging that whatever the cause of their suffering, justice requires that one come to their aid.

Why these resistances? Why resistance to acknowledging that the plight of the suffering is the consequence of injustice—and hence resistance to supporting the struggle for the righting of the injustice? Because the struggle to right injustice almost always produces conflict with those responsible for the injustice; not infrequently it is not only conflictual but dangerous. If one ignores the injustice of the situation and concentrates on alleviating the plight of the suffering, one makes no accusations and engenders no conflict. The malefactors can continue doing what they were doing without having accusations thrown at them; indeed, they are now more free than they were before to continue doing what they were doing, since now the plight of their victims has been alleviated and their cries are less wrenching.

And why resistance to acknowledging that, whatever the cause of their suffering, justice requires that one come to the aid of those with whom one emphasizes? Because benevolence is morally optional. If justice does not require that I give clothes that my children have outgrown to the African family living in my backyard, if I would not wrong them if I did not give them clothes, then it's up to me to decide whether or not to do so. I'm in charge. I can call the shots. And I can set conditions on my benevolence, including the condition that the recipients express gratitude. But if justice requires that I give clothes to the family, if I would wrong them if I did not, then it's not morally optional for me. I am morally obligated to give the clothes; it is morally impermissible for me not to do so. I'm not in charge. I am, as it were, decentered.

The two reasons I have just now mentioned, for resistance to allowing one's empathy to lead one to answer the call for justice, are common to human beings in general. We all prefer to avoid conflict and danger; we all prefer to be in charge. If we now recall our earlier discussion about the relation between justice and love, then we see that there is a third reason for resistance that is peculiar to Christians. If one interprets the New Testament as supplanting justice with love, then of course one will resist ever interpreting the situation before one as calling for the doing of justice or for lending one's support to the struggle for righting injustice. One will instead interpret every situation as calling for a benevolent love that pays no attention to what justice requires.

I have been reflecting in this chapter on why it is that seeing the faces and hearing the voices of the victims of systemic injustice sometimes evokes no empathy for the victims, and sometimes evokes empathy but no recognition of the call to do justice and to support the struggle for the righting of injustice.

Now recall the theory of primary justice that I sketched out earlier. I suggested that justice is grounded in rights; a society is just insofar as its members are treated as they have a right to be treated. And I suggested that rights are grounded in the worth, the excellence, the dignity, the estimability, of those human beings who are the rights-bearers. I have a right to the good of being treated a certain way if that's what is required for being treated as befits my worth. Rights are to those ways of being treated that due respect for worth requires.

Whatever be the reason in a given case for the fact that seeing the faces and hearing the voices of victims of injustice either evokes no empathy, or evokes an empathy that ignores or resists the call to do justice and to support the struggle for the righting of injustice, what is missing is due recognition of the dignity of the victims. In those benevolent Afrikaners there was no recognition of the dignity of the Africans living in their backyards, and thus no recognition of the fact that the economic and political system that made them live as dependents in their backyards was a violation of their dignity. They thought only in terms of doing good to them, improving their lives in some small way. They did not recognize that their dignity was being violated.

Shortly after the publication of my book *Justice: Rights and Wrongs*, I had a conversation with a sociologist from Queens University, Belfast. He said he had read the book with great interest. He especially liked my grounding of rights in dignity; he thought that that was a much more promising way to go than trying to ground them in autonomy. After a few more such complimentary comments he went on to say that he wanted to suggest that I should now write a sequel in which I discussed what can be done to get people to acknowledge the dignity of their fellow human beings, to recognize when that dignity is being violated, and to act accordingly.

I have not written that book. A person trained as a philosopher, such as myself, is not equipped to write such a book. A well-grounded book on the topic would employ the resources of sociological and psychological theory and be thoroughly versed in the great social justice movements of the past couple of centuries: the movement in nineteenth-century England for the abolition of the slave trade, the antislavery movement in nineteenth-century America, the labor rights movement in the United States and other countries in the early twentieth century, the American civil rights movement in the mid-twentieth century, the anti-apartheid movement in South Africa. It would also be versed in more narrowly focused social justice movements such as those described by Jeffrey Stout in his fine book *Blessed Are the Organized*.

With these resources in hand, the writer of the book would then develop a structural analysis of social justice movements in general, keeping in mind the questions posed to me: What can be done to get people to acknowledge the dignity of their fellow human beings, to recognize when that dignity is being violated, and to act accordingly?

❖ 24 ❖

The Structure
of Social Justice Movements

At the end of the preceding chapter I spoke of a structural analysis of social justice movements that was thoroughly informed by psychological and sociological theory and based on a detailed study of some of the great social justice movements of the past two centuries. I added that a philosopher such as myself is not equipped to construct such an analysis. My knowledge of psychological and sociological theory is too skimpy, my historical knowledge too limited.

As will be evident from the preceding pages, however, I am not completely ignorant of social justice movements. I was a supporter and close observer of the civil rights movement in the United States. I was a supporter and close observer of the anti-apartheid movement in South Africa; at one point I played a small part in the movement. I have recently read Adam Hochschild's marvelous book *Bury the Chains*, on the movement in early nineteenth-century England to abolish the slave trade. I have read Jeffrey Stout's description, in *Blessed Are the Organized: Grassroots Democracy in America*, of what he calls "broad-based organizing";[1] most of Stout's examples are of actions undertaken by affiliates of the Industrial Areas Foundation, a confederation of community organizations in the United States founded in 1940 by Saul Alinsky. I have followed the work of the International Justice Mission, aimed at stopping sex trafficking and slave labor in various parts of the world. I have observed at first hand the work of the Association for a More Just Society in Honduras. In short, my knowledge of social justice movements is a good deal more than impressionistic. But it is not deep. The structural analysis that I will now be so bold as to propose is, accordingly, tentative, and perhaps amateurish. And it does not apply—not without adaptation—to situations such as that in Northern Ireland before the Good Friday Agreement, where everybody was a victim or under the threat of becoming a victim.

Let me explain what I take social justice movements and organizations to be. Wronging comes in many forms. You are wronged if someone invades your privacy for prurient reasons; you are wronged if the receptionist in the health clinic insults you. Such wrongings, important though they often are for the one who is wronged, are not the concern of social justice movements and organizations. Social justice movements and organizations are concerned with those wrongings that are the result of public social practices, of laws, or of how the laws are enforced or not enforced. Their goal is to right those sorts of wrongings.

It will prove helpful to note and keep in mind the distinction, among social justice movements and organizations, between those whose members are mainly the *victims* of some social injustice, and those whose members are mainly *supporters* of the victims. Let me call these, respectively, *victim movements and organizations*, and *supporter movements and organizations*. The anti-apartheid movement in South Africa was an example of the former; the movement in nineteenth-century England for the abolition of the slave trade

1. Jeffrey Stout, *Blessed Are the Organized: Grassroots Democracy in America* (Princeton: Princeton University Press, 2010).

was an example of the latter, as are the Honduran Association for a More Just Society and the International Justice Movement. The mid-twentieth-century civil rights movement in the United States was a movement whose members were almost equally victims of racial discrimination and supporters of the victims.

The fact that social justice movements and organizations are concerned with the righting of injustice that is the result of public social practices, of laws, or of how the laws are enforced or not enforced explains why often they do not name very many names. The first great social justice critics in the Western tradition were the Old Testament prophets. Here is a typical passage from Isaiah. The prophet is excoriating those

> who make iniquitous decrees,
>   who write oppressive statutes,
> to turn aside the needy from justice
>   and to rob the poor of my people of their right,
> that widows may be [their] spoil
>   and that [they] may make the orphans [their] prey!
>   (10:1–2 NRSV)

The prophet names no names, cites no examples. He and the other prophets did not hesitate to point the finger when the occasion demanded; witness the prophet Nathan confronting King David, for his affair with Bathsheba, with the accusing words, "You are the man!" (2 Sam. 12:7). But the target of Isaiah's attack, in this and similar passages, is not specific episodes of injustice and specific wrongdoers but those public social practices, those laws, or those ways of enforcing or not enforcing the laws, whose effect was to turn aside widows, orphans, and the poor from justice and rob them of their right. Isaiah's concern is the righting of social injustice.

To recognize social injustice one must be able to look beyond particular episodes of victimization, and beyond particular victims, to recognize a certain similarity in a number of episodes. That done, one must then be able to look behind that similarity to discern what accounts for it—namely, certain public social practices, certain laws, or certain ways of enforcing or not enforcing those laws. This latter ability, the ability to discern the cause of the pattern of victimization, requires the ability to engage in a certain sort of abstraction. To determine whether someone is a participant in a public social practice that wreaks widespread victimization, or responsible for a law or some way of enforcing or not enforcing a law that wreaks widespread victimization, one must be able to abstract from his or her conscious intentions.

Some people find it difficult, both in their own case and in the case of others, to perform this sort of abstraction. This is not how they normally think. Others find it not so much difficult to think this way as offensive to be told that they and their friends are responsible for suffering. They are good people with the best of intentions. They contribute generously to the benevolence fund of their church. How can they possibly be guilty of causing anybody to suffer? Yet others resist this sort of abstraction as an irrelevant distraction. What a person does is shaped by where the person's heart lies; it's a distraction to talk about social practices.

Social justice movements almost always require a considerable length of time to achieve their goal, and almost always they require leaders. I dare say that a full history of social justice movements would uncover a few cases in which there was a spontaneous outburst of outrage that achieved almost instantaneous success, but those are the exceptions.

Let me now identify and describe what I shall call the *stages* of social justice movements. The term "stages" suggests temporal sequence. But what I identify as *stages* may or may not occur in sequence; often several occur more or less simultaneously.

Every social justice movement begins with the identification of *victims* of public social practices, of laws, or of ways of enforcing or not enforcing those laws. The end-goal of the movement is to get those who engage in those public social practices, or who are responsible for those laws or for how they are enforced or not enforced, to cease and desist from what they are doing; a complementary goal is to get their defenders to cease and desist from defending them.

This goal, of getting the victimizers and their defenders to cease and desist from what they are doing, requires that the victimizers and their defenders be aware of the plight of the victims and be aware of the ways in which they are contributing to their plight. Sometimes the victimizers and their defenders are already fully aware of these. Usually, though, that plight is wholly or partly concealed from them, as are its causes in their own actions. They live in gated communities; they never set foot in a ghetto. They live in Israel proper; they never set foot in a West Bank Palestinian village. When the victimizers and their defenders suffer from this sort of oblivion, the leaders of the social justice movement aim at awakening them to the plight of the victims and its causes.

If the movement is in whole or in part a victim movement, the leaders of the movement may also find it necessary to induce an awakening in the victims. Individual victims will usually be aware of their own plight. But often they have little knowledge of the extent to which their plight is shared, and often they have scant knowledge of the cause of their plight and that of others. Information coupled with social analysis is required. A crucial initial stage in all the movements that Jeffrey Stout describes in his book was an awakening of the victims to the cause and extent of what was going on.

If the movement is a supporter movement, or both a victim and a supporter movement, it will usually also be necessary for the leaders to induce an awakening in the public, since usually the public will be ignorant of the social injustice at issue or ignorant of its extent. Here too, information coupled with social analysis is required. By "the public" I mean those who are neither the direct victims of the social injustice at issue nor the victimizers and their defenders. The public that the leaders aim to enlist as supporters may belong to the same society as that in which the social injustice is occurring, or they may not. The leaders of the movement for the abolition of the slave trade between Africa and the Americas aimed at enlisting the public in England as supporters. When the movement began, very few members of the English public knew anything about the trade or about the condition of the slaves; essential to the success of the movement was the extraordinary widespread awakening that it eventually achieved. My own speaking and writing about the situation in South Africa and the Middle East was my attempt, in cooperation with others, to awaken the American public to the social injustice that was occurring there.

Mere knowledge of the plight of the victims and its causes is not sufficient, however; awakening is not enough. The awakening must be accompanied by an emotional response. In the ideal case, the victimizers and their defenders respond to their awakening with empathy for the victims and regret for their own complicity in the victims' plight. Seldom does that happen, however. In its absence, what is needed, if the movement is a victim movement, is emotional grievance on the part of the victims at what is being done to them and anger at those who are doing it; if the movement is a supporter movement, what is needed is empathy with the victims along with emotional grievance and anger. Unless there are those whose empathy and anger move them to cry out, "This must not be," nothing will change. Information and social analysis are not yet social action. Action requires emotional engagement. It was my empathy with the Palestinians and the so-called blacks and coloreds in South Africa, coupled with the anger I felt toward their victimizers, that spurred me to action.

If my own case was typical, news reports of what is happening will seldom be sufficient to generate the necessary emotional engagement in the public. The victims and their plight must somehow be made vivid to people—by face-to-face encounters, by personal stories, by film, by fiction.

In the preceding chapter I took note of some of the factors that block empathy and harden hearts. One or more of these factors will typically be at work in the victimizers and their defenders; often they will be at work in significant parts of the general public as well. The public as well as the victimizers and their defenders discern that empathetic response to the victims might well lead to feeling compelled to make changes in one's behavior that would not be in one's perceived self-interest; the public as well as the victimizers and their defenders have learned to dehumanize the victims or ascribe to them no more than a diminished humanity; the public as well as the victimizers and their defenders have embraced a narrative that says that the plight of the victims is of their own making; the public as well as the victimizers and their defenders have embraced a visionary ideology that says that the plight of the victims is the regrettable side effect of a great good that beckons.

Social justice movements and organizations have to deal with these blockages to empathy; each has to craft its way of dealing with them to the particularities of its situation. Defenders of the slave trade loudly and insistently claimed that the elimination of the trade would have severe economic consequences in England; on Hochschild's telling, the abolition movement worked hard at combating this claim. A good many of the narratives concerning events surrounding the founding of the state of Israel and concerning its diplomatic practices claim that the plight of the Palestinians is of their own making; in recent years a number of Israeli historians have shown in detail how false and distorted these narratives are.[2]

It appears to me that the most difficult blockages to undo are those caused by the demeaning of the victims or by the embrace of a visionary ideology that justifies what is being done. How does one get a people to give up the inspirational vision of a great day in the future to be achieved by all together following their leaders and pushing aside the softhearted? How does one get one group of human beings to acknowledge the human dignity of another group, when demeaning prejudice has entered into the very fabric of their souls? Liberal thinkers have often suggested that if we can get members of the hostile groups to live and work together in situations of equality, demeaning discrimination will disappear. However, I am told that, for some time, the effect of eliminating racial segregation in the US armed forces was not that the prejudice of whites against African Americans melted away but that whites viewed their prejudices as confirmed.

2. See, for example, Avi Shlaim, *The Iron Wall: Israel and the Arab World* (New York: Norton, 2001).

After awakening and emotional engagement, the third stage is *activation*. The victims, if it is a victim movement, must be activated to do something to get the victimizers and their defenders to cease and desist; the supporters, if it is a supporter movement, must likewise be activated. Leaders are once again indispensable. They do essentially five things: they inspire their followers by imagining a future in which things are different, they persuade them that such a future is attainable, they offer concrete suggestions for actions that can be taken to bring about that future, they organize and mobilize their followers to engage in those actions, and, since those whom they organize and mobilize often have no prior affinity for one another, they cultivate emotional solidarity among members of the movement. Martin Luther King Jr. was a genius at all five of these.

Though the Hebrew prophets did not offer practical advice to social reformers, they did do what is indispensable to all social justice movements: they insisted that things do not have to be as they are, and they imagined a society in which things were different. The extant laws and practices are not laws of nature ordained by God; neither do they express the ineluctable laws of the marketplace or the unalterable preconditions of social order. The widows, the orphans, the aliens, and the impoverished are not social unfortunates about whose condition nothing can be done; they are the victims of laws and public social practices that can be changed. The prophets describe them as downtrodden. It is sometimes said that not until the early modern period did people in general believe that social structures and practices are human constructs that can be changed. It seems to me indubitable that the Hebrew prophets already believed that.

Some of the most lyrically visionary passages in all of Western literature are expressions of the social imagination of the Hebrew prophets. The prophet imagines a day when the bonds of wickedness are loosed and the thongs of the yoke are undone, when the oppressed are let free and every yoke is broken, when people share their bread with the hungry, take the homeless poor into their houses, clothe the naked, and do not avert their eyes from their own kin (Isa. 58:6–7).

The great "I Have a Dream" speech of Martin Luther King Jr. was a noble successor in the tradition of prophetic social imagination.

The leaders of social justice movements often find that their proposals for organizing and mobilizing their followers to actions that promise to right the social injustice fall on deaf ears because a culture of passivity has captured the victims and significant sections of the public. The victims understand their situation and are angry at their oppressors; but they have sunk into resigned passivity. The public knows the facts and feels empathy for the victims and anger at their victimizers, but they wallow in anguished hand-wringing. Sometimes the cause of this culture of passivity is pervasive corruption: both victims and the general public believe that corruption is so pervasive among those who hold power that any attempt to right the injustice will get nowhere. Sometimes the cause of the culture of passivity is the failure of all previous attempts to right the injustice.

As we will see in the next chapter, social justice movements in Honduras bump up against a culture of passivity, both in victims and in the general public. The main cause seems to be twofold. Pervasive in Honduran society are distrust and fear: victims of crime distrust and fear the police, the police fear the criminals and distrust the prosecutors, the prosecutors fear the criminals and distrust the police, victims distrust and fear their neighbors. In this situation there is of course corruption, as one would expect; but those who work in social justice movements in Honduras believe that the cause of passivity goes deeper than corruption; it is the pervasive distrust and fear. In addition, large segments of the public have adopted a theology that enjoins passivity; the pervasive distrust and fear lend social plausibility to the theology.

When victims and the public have sunk into social passivity, attempts by leaders to activate them will obviously get nowhere unless the culture of passivity is forthrightly addressed and dealt with. Whether it be a victim movement or a supporter movement, people must come to believe that something *can* be done, that things *can* be different.

Evoking an awakening to the plight of the victims and its causes, evoking an emotional engagement with the victims and their victimizers, and activating the victims or some segment of the public to engage in actions that will cause the victimizers and their defenders to cease and desist—these actions can all be urged by their leaders and performed by their followers without employing moral concepts. (The initial stages of the movements that Jeffrey Stout describes in his book often did not employ moral concepts.) I have quite deliberately described the three stages of social justice movements that I have identified—awakening, emotional engagement, and activation—without using moral concepts. The central concept in my analysis has been that of *victim*, not that of oppressed. Victim is not a moral concept; neither are the concepts of grievance, anger, and regret.

Alternatively, the three stages that I have identified can be urged by the leaders and performed by their followers with moral concepts other than those of rights, wrongs, justice, and so forth. They can be urged and employed using the concepts of benevolence, charity, and the like.

All social justice movements and organizations must at some point take the step of offering a *social justice analysis and critique* of the situation. The victims are not just suffering, as would be the case had a tornado hit or a volcano erupted. Nor are they just social unfortunates. Their condition has the specific form of their being subjects of injustice; they are wronged, wronged by those who are their victimizers. They are oppressed, downtrodden. The social analysis of the Hebrew prophets always took the form of social justice analysis and critique.

In order to offer a social justice analysis and critique, social justice movements obviously need some idea of what justice is, some idea of what rights are, and an ability to discern when rights are being violated. This is where I see most of my own writing about justice as making a contribution.

Sometimes the injustice leaps out to everybody. When the police in Honduras refuse to investigate crimes because they fear that the perpetrators will "get even" with them, it leaps out to everybody that they are wronging those who have already been wronged. When the International Justice Mission uncovers cases of sex trafficking and slave labor, it leaps out to everybody that wrong is being done to young women and children.

But injustice doesn't always leap out. Usually it leaps out to the victims, but sometimes it does not leap out to the oppressors and their defenders, nor to the public. Sometimes it does not leap out because the oppressors, their defenders, and the public have embraced an analysis of the situation that concludes that it is not a case of injustice. Sometimes it does not leap out because the situation is complex, and it's not obvious that injustice is involved; the social justice analysis and critique required to bring the injustice to light has not been done or is not widely available. Social justice analysis and critique is one of the principal contributions that scholars can make to the work of social justice movements and organizations.

What I have said so far may give the impression that social justice movements are rather genteel and leisurely undertakings. They aim at producing an awakening to the plight of the victims and its causes. They aim at evoking an emotional engagement with the victims and their victimizers. They aim at activating the victims and/or their supporters to take steps to get the victimizers and their defenders to cease and desist. And they offer a social justice analysis and critique of the situation. All quite genteel.

But social justice movements are hardly ever genteel. Almost always they are laced through with conflict, hostility, and resistance. Almost always they require a great deal of courage on the part of the participants. Nobody is against relief organizations. Nobody is against development organizations, provided the development in question genuinely contributes to the well-being of the people. But social justice movements and organizations get under people's skin. They get people angry. Blessed are those who are persecuted because they seek justice, said Jesus.

It is especially at the activation stage that conflict, hostility, and resistance erupt. To claim that certain public social practices, certain laws, or certain ways of enforcing or not enforcing those laws are unjust is to launch a moral critique against those who are responsible for these. That critique almost always evokes not just disagreement but anger in those against whom the moral critique is launched. But now, when the leaders move beyond social justice critique to activating their followers, they encounter more than disagreement; they encounter hostility and resistance. Almost always the attempt of the leaders of the movement at persuasion fails; the oppressors refuse to cease and desist. They dig in their heels. Now the movement has no choice but to move beyond persuasion and put pressure on them—pressure aimed at changing the situation so that the self-interest of the oppressors and their defenders now lies in changing things. Strategic imagination on the part of the leaders is required at this point. Not infrequently resistance to pressure takes the form of violence; sometimes the pressure itself takes the form of violence.

First the oppressors and their defenders resist the pressure, perhaps with lethal force. But if the movement is successful, eventually they find themselves forced to give way. Previously their self-interest lay in keeping things as they are; now it lies in giving in to the demands of the protestors. They may have no more empathy for the victims now than they did before. They may continue to insist that no injustice is being done. But what lies in their self-interest has now changed.

The campaign for divesting in corporations that did business in South Africa is a good example of the point: the campaign succeeded in making it no longer in the interest of the South African government to perpetuate apartheid. The stories about social justice movements that Jeffrey Stout tells in *Blessed Are the Organized* are all stories about pressure being brought on the oppressors so that it was no longer in their interest to continue doing what they were doing.

Social justice movements typically produce conflict and hostility not only between the movement and the oppressors but also within the public. Almost always it turns out that there are members of the public who disagree with the social justice critique being lodged by the leaders of the movement. But usually there will also be those who agree with the critique but oppose what the leaders of the social justice movement are doing to try to change things. They argue for other strategies. Or they argue that the desired change should be allowed to come about in an evolutionary way.

It is at the activation stage that conflict typically also erupts within the movement itself. Members of the movement disagree over the details of the new order that the movement should aim at. What some hold out as desirable, others argue is not desirable; what some hold out as possible, others argue is not possible. They disagree over the compromises they should be willing to accept. And they disagree over the tactics that the movement should employ for bringing about the new order. Some argue for violence; others warn against violence.

I mentioned earlier that social justice movements almost always require leaders and almost always take a long time to achieve the desired result. The story of almost every social justice movement is a story not only of courage but of extraordinary steadfastness on the part of leaders and followers alike. In the midst of conflict, hostility, and resistance in all directions, the leaders must keep alive the cry "This must not be," they must inspire their followers with the vision of a new order, they must build solidarity, and they must maintain hope within themselves and their followers. How they do this deserves an essay of its own. Let me make just three brief closing observations.

Keeping alive the memory of some egregious outrage often proves important for keeping alive the cry "This must not be." The resistance movement in South Africa kept alive the memory of the massacre in Sharpeville with the cry "Remember Sharpeville." The Palestinians continue to keep alive the memory of the calamity that befell them, after the recognition of the state of Israel by the United Nations, when they were terrorized into leaving their ancestral lands and villages.

Second, in a good many social justice movements, songs and chants play an important role in building solidarity. That was the role played in the South African resistance movement by the chant "Die oumas, die oupas. . . ." And that was the role played in the American civil rights movement by the song "We Shall Overcome."

Third, in a good many social justice movements, worship plays an indispensable role in building solidarity and keeping hope alive. That was the case in the American civil rights movement; it was likewise the case in the South African resistance movement.

PART 5

JUST PUNISHMENT

❖ 25 ❖

A Visit to Honduras

In chapter 4 I distinguished two fundamentally different types of rights, *reactive rights* and *primary rights*. Corresponding to these two kinds of rights are two kinds of justice, *reactive justice* and *primary justice*.

In the cry for justice by the people of color in South Africa and by the Palestinians, I heard a cry for the doing of primary justice and for the righting of primary injustice. I did not hear a cry for criminal justice, nor indeed for any other kind of reactive justice. A reliable rule of thumb for listening to American politicians is that if the politician talks about justice, assume that he or she is talking about criminal justice; assume that he or she is talking about punishment, prisons, and the like. The people of color in South Africa and the Palestinians were not crying out for criminal justice. I think it was because my reflections on justice were spurred and shaped by my encounter with these people that my writings on justice focused almost entirely on primary justice.

It was another trip to the global South, this one very recent, that brought home to me that in the absence of reactive justice in general, and criminal justice in particular, primary justice is inevitably impaired. Following is a slight revision of what I wrote about my trip.[1]

I touched down in Tegucigalpa, the capital of Honduras, around noon on Saturday, March 20, 2010. For several years Kurt Ver Beek had been urging me to come and witness firsthand the work of la Asociación para una Sociedad más Justa (Association for a More Just Society), abbreviated as ASJ. Now finally the opportunity to do so had opened up. I was joined by a few other visitors from the United States.

ASJ is a Christian organization. Most readers will be aware of North American Christian organizations doing relief or development work in various parts of the so-called Third World, World Vision being the largest and perhaps the best known of these. Some will also be aware of North American Christian organizations engaged in the struggle against one or another form of injustice in the Third World, International Justice Mission (IJM) being the largest of these. ASJ is like IJM in that it is a justice organization rather than a relief or development organization; it is unlike IJM in that it is a Honduran organization. It was founded in 2000 by Ver Beek and five others, four of them native Hondurans; its staff has always been almost entirely Honduran, and its leadership is now entirely Honduran. The association now has some fifty-five people on its staff, about three-quarters of them women.

Over the course of my five-day visit I was moved and inspired by the dedication, tenacity, imagination, and courage displayed by the staff and leadership of ASJ. I was also fascinated by the way in which the association has crafted its struggle against injustice to the particularities of Honduran society—particularities very different from those of North American society. And I was intrigued by the distinct understanding of the task of the state that was implicit in the work

1. My report was published under the title "Just Demands" in *The Christian Century* 127, no. 15, July 27, 2010, 30–34. It was reprinted, with a few revisions, in my *Hearing the Call* (Grand Rapids: Eerdmans, 2011).

of the association and by what it was doing to get the state to carry out its task, particularly with respect to the poor.

The association has three major projects: the Peace and Justice Project, which is a victims' rights program, the Labor Rights Project, and the Land Rights Project. (Be it noticed that ASJ is not shy of using the word *rights*.) Each morning the person or persons in charge of one of the projects described their project to us; then in the afternoon we went out into the field.

The Peace and Justice Project provides investigative, legal, and psychological aid to poor victims of violent crime and assists under-equipped, underfinanced, overworked, and frightened government officials in carrying out their responsibilities toward these victims; when necessary, it prods officials to carry out their responsibilities. On the first weekday morning of our visit, the head of the Peace and Justice Project described its work. What he said set the stage for the descriptions of the other projects as well.

He observed that it is commonly said that the failure of Honduran officials to deal with crime against the poor is due to corruption—graft and bribery. Both he and Kurt argued, however, that though there are indeed corrupt officials, the fundamental problem is not corruption but fear and a pervasive lack of trust. Poor people do not trust the police, the judicial system, or the bureaucracy. The police do not trust the prosecutors; the prosecutors do not trust the police. The result is that the poor are afraid to take action when they are the victims of crime or illegal treatment; they fear that if they file a report with the police or some government official, the person or organization that wronged them will retaliate. The police and prosecutors likewise fear that they will be the victims of retaliation if they take action. There is plenty of evidence that these fears are warranted. What I saw, more clearly than ever before, is that justice in all its forms is impossible in the midst of pervasive fear and distrust.

A missionary with whom I talked described the Hondurans as the most passive people he had ever encountered; he had previously worked in the Dominican Republic and Haiti. By the end of my visit

I concluded that describing the Hondurans as passive is not on target. Nor is it correct to describe them as simply accepting the wrongs done to them. Though they put up with them, they do not cease to say, "This should not be." Better to describe them as believing that, because government cannot be trusted, there's nothing to be done in bringing to justice those who have wronged them.

I leave it to historians to explain how this climate of distrust developed. Discussions later in the week made clear, however, that the theology dominant in the churches, both Protestant and Catholic, is intertwined with the ingrained habit of doing nothing when one is victimized. Paul's injunction in Romans 12:19, "Never avenge yourselves, but leave room for the wrath of God; for it is written, 'Vengeance is mine, I will repay, says the Lord,'" is widely interpreted as meaning that it is not the business of Christians to bring those who perpetrate crimes and violate the law to the bar of earthly justice; meting out justice is God's business. In the final judgment, God will punish those who perpetrate crimes and violate the law, and reward those who patiently put up with the wrongs done to them; it is not for us to undertake God's work. This otherworldly theology supports the habit of putting up with the wrongs done to one because government cannot be trusted; conversely, the social habit gives relevance to the theology.

The Peace and Justice Project has targeted two of the impoverished neighborhoods in Tegucigalpa, one of thirty thousand and the other of seventy thousand inhabitants, as places where it will stand alongside the victims of violent crime. When the police in these neighborhoods refuse or decline to investigate crime, whether because of lack of resources or fear of reprisal by criminals, and when witnesses refuse out of fear to testify, ASJ has stepped in to conduct investigations (the police have to verify the information and make arrests). It has assisted prosecutors in preparing criminal cases. And when witnesses are fearful of testifying in court, ASJ has employed a recourse allowed in Honduran law of "protected witnesses." Witnesses to a crime appear in court hooded from head to foot; as they testify, their voices are technologically altered.

In the six years that the Peace and Justice Project has been operating, it has played a significant, often decisive, role in the conviction of more than one hundred perpetrators of crime. Homicides in the targeted neighborhoods have been reduced from forty-two in 2005 to nine in 2009; over the same period, the number of homicides throughout Honduras has more than doubled, from 2,155 to 5,012.

In the afternoon we were driven up into one of the targeted neighborhoods, Villa Nueva, and invited into a neat, clean, small living room. Two women spoke of the rape of their daughters and told of how the police declined to do anything until ASJ intervened; the perpetrators were discovered, apprehended, and convicted. A young man spoke of being shot and wounded and of how, in his case too, the police declined to do anything until ASJ intervened; the perpetrators were then identified, apprehended, and convicted. There were no dry eyes in the crowded room.

The next day the head of the Labor Rights Project described for us the work of her project. In 1954 Honduras instituted a progressive set of labor laws, this the outcome of a massive labor strike against two US banana companies. When it comes to poor workers, however, the laws are often not enforced, partly because of woefully inadequate resources for government investigators, partly out of fear on the part of investigators and prosecutors, and partly because workers fear that, if they file a complaint, they will either become the victim of reprisals or be arbitrarily fired. (The high rate of unemployment means that there are always others to take the place of those who are fired.) ASJ has concentrated its efforts on two of the most abused groups, cleaning workers and security guards. The association has now educated more than 7,000 workers on their rights and has been instrumental in winning cases for 135.

A number of companies in Honduras offer security guards on contract to organizations and individuals. Among these, one of the most notorious for its treatment of employees is Setech. Setech employees are sometimes not paid for months at a time, forced to work twenty-four-hour shifts, not paid overtime, arbitrarily fired, and so forth.

Dionisio Diaz Garcia was one of the ASJ lawyers assigned to investigate the practices of Setech and other security and cleaning companies; he managed to bring a good many systematic violations of the labor laws to the attention of the relevant authorities. On December 4, 2006, Dionisio was assassinated as he was headed for court to participate in a hearing involving security guards. Two men on a motorcycle pulled up alongside his car on a busy street in Tegucigalpa, one of them shot Dionisio at point-blank range, and they sped off. Kurt told me that upon hearing the news, he fully expected most of the staff of ASJ to resign; the work was just too dangerous. Only one person left. This is part of what I had in mind when I spoke of the courage of the staff and leaders of ASJ.

Though the assassination of Dionisio occurred in broad daylight and was witnessed by a good many people, some in other cars, some sitting alongside the road selling things, it was only with great difficulty that ASJ was able to get any of the eyewitnesses to talk. Eventually a few did, and the perpetrators were identified and apprehended. Both had worked for the Setech organization; the driver of the motorcycle was an active police officer at the time of the killing. Two of the witnesses testified as "protected witnesses" at the trial. The court found their testimony credible, and the two men were convicted of murder and sentenced to jail. ASJ is now working to help and prod Honduran justice authorities to identify and bring to justice the brains behind the assassination.

After the head of the Labor Rights Project had finished her presentation, we went out into the field. First we visited an eleven-hundred-bed public hospital whose patients consist almost exclusively of the very poor; the care is free. We tried to engage some of the cleaning women in conversation; they refused to say anything. ASJ learned recently that they had been told by the company that if they were caught talking to anybody about how they were treated, they would be summarily fired. Shortly one of the top managers of the hospital appeared. He showed us around the hospital, and explained to us that one of his biggest problems was "the attitude," as he called it, of some of the workers.

The hospital is surrounded by a high security fence; the gates were tended by guards wearing Setech uniforms. As we were waiting for our van to arrive, we found two guards who were willing to talk. Both told us that they were regularly forced to work twenty-four-hour shifts. One said that he had not been paid for more than a month, the other, that he had not been paid for three months. When we asked whether this happened often, they said it did. When we asked whether the company eventually gave them their back pay, they said that sometimes it did and sometimes it did not. Both were middle-aged men with families; the one who said he had not been paid for three months said he had seven children. Why had they lost their fear of talking to strangers? That never became clear.

We left the hospital to go to the attorney general's office. There we met with the head of the division dealing with human rights violations, with the head of the division dealing with crimes against children, and with the director of the prosecutors in the Dionisio case. They expressed their gratitude for the many ways in which ASJ had been of assistance to them: conducting investigations, finding witnesses, encouraging witnesses to testify, lending the prosecutors cars when they found themselves without transportation, and so forth. It became clear in the course of the discussion, however, that ASJ was by no means a lapdog for the government. The ASJ representatives declared that they too appreciated the level of cooperation between their staff and that of the attorney general's office; but they also made clear that they would continue to file complaints, both verbal and written, when they found officials negligent in carrying out their responsibilities. The people from the attorney general's office nodded to indicate that they were well aware of this! I was struck by the large number of women in the upper echelons of the attorney general's staff. Someone remarked that women are in general more courageous than men.

It was in the course of these discussions in the attorney general's office that there came into focus for me the distinctive stance of ASJ toward government. The implicit assumption in everything ASJ does is that it is the task of government to secure justice in society by instituting a system of just laws, by effectively and justly enforcing those laws, and by meting out justice to those who violate the laws. Given this assumption, ASJ then does three things: it stands alongside the victims and defends their cause, it holds government officials responsible for enforcing the laws and finding and punishing violators, and it assists the officials in carrying out this task. On the last two points: the association does not try to execute an end run around government, nor does it content itself with dispensing aid and charity to victims; it holds government officials responsible. Neither does it content itself with issuing denunciations; it assists officials in carrying out their task.

Let me jump ahead a bit. The last afternoon of my visit we attended a meeting of ASJ representatives with the head of a large grocery chain and the head of the firm that does cleaning work on contract for the chain. ASJ had been publicizing and protesting some of the abusive ways in which the cleaning firm treated its workers; a sixty-year-old cleaning woman who had been ordered to take a pregnancy test or be fired had come along with the ASJ team.

The head of the cleaning firm was very angry. I will quote, without comment, some of the English translation of what he said:

> People in Honduras are always playing the victim. You should have asked my permission before you talked to my workers. There are always people who complain. I've got rights too. Why don't you talk about my rights, why do you only talk about their rights? The Bible tells us to love our neighbors. I'm loving these people by giving them jobs. Let's talk about Christian principles. I'm using my talents. The Bible says that those who are given many talents must use them. I was given many talents. We all have the right to get more than we have. Let the state regulate what I do; you stay out of it. I'm not going to let anybody tell me how to run my company. Leave me alone. I can sue you for slander. I insist on the freedom to do what I want to do. I don't owe anybody any explanations.

On the third morning, three of the leaders of the Land Rights Project described their work for us. Tegucigalpa is built on a series of steep ridges; over the past thirty years or so there has been a large influx of poor people who have built houses on outlying ridges. Ownership of the land on which they built was often obscure or contested. Though they always paid someone for their plot of land, it was often not clear whether they were paying the right party. Sometimes they did not receive a title even though they paid the asking price; sometimes the title they received proved invalid.

Five years ago the government passed a land reform act. The details of how the act works need not concern us. Suffice it to say that large landowners who can establish ownership wind up with a fair price, and residents, after paying a fair price for their plots or establishing that they have already paid a fair price, are given clear title to their plot. ASJ has assisted some sixty thousand poor families in the Tegucigalpa and San Pedro Sula areas in getting clear title to their plots.

Our field trip in the afternoon consisted of going up into one of the neighborhoods, Los Centenos, where ASJ has been instrumental in helping the people get their titles. The residents were immensely proud of these titles; they displayed them, asked to be photographed holding them, and so on. But what I found just as impressive and moving was something that the three leaders of the Land Rights Project had taken for granted and neglected to mention to us. The area we visited contained four distinct communities. We learned that whereas the city installed water, sewer, and electrical systems in middle-class neighborhoods, each of these poor communities had to install these systems on its own. In order to do so, and to deal with other business, each had instituted an organizational structure with a president, a vice president, a secretary, and a treasurer. Candidates were nominated for these offices, and the community held elections. Women were prominent among the officers. This was small-scale democracy at work. This was activity, not passivity. I asked two of the male vice presidents leading us around what they did for a living. One said that he was a security guard, the other said that he was retired from being a security guard. I did not ask which firm they worked for. I wish I had.

My visit was too short; I left Honduras on Thursday. But my impressions were vivid and my memories are indelible. I had seen the faces and heard the voices of some of the wronged and vulnerable in Honduras; I had been moved to empathetic identification. I had witnessed firsthand the work of an indigenous organization that, with great tenacity, courage, and imagination, insists that the government bring lawbreakers to justice and assists it in doing so. And I had been brought to realize, what now seems obvious, that without a just and effective system of criminal justice, the struggle for primary justice and for the righting of primary injustice will get nowhere.

❖ 26 ❖

St. Paul's Rejection of Retributive Punishment

ASJ is a social justice organization, not a relief or development organization. Implicit in how it works is the assumption that the state is the primary institution in society for securing justice. ASJ does not confine itself to binding up the wounds of victims of injustice—though it does some of that. It does not try to do an end run around government by setting up parallel institutions, such as schools, when the government fails in its task. It does not content itself with launching denunciatory preachments at the government. It prods government to do what government is supposed to do—namely, secure justice in society—and it assists government in doing that.

In acting thus, ASJ is reflecting a profoundly Pauline understanding of the God-given task of the state. Let me substantiate this claim by looking at what Paul says in the last five verses of chapter 12 of his Letter to the Romans and in the first seven verses of chapter 13. Over the centuries, this passage in Paul's Letter to the Romans has evoked a great deal of political passivity in Christians; it continues to do so today. I hold that that rests on a misunderstanding of what Paul is saying.

The traditional interpretation has two main components. One component is the claim that the God-given task of government is to impose retributive punishment on wrongdoers. The other component consists of the conjunction of three claims: whatever be the government of a certain group of people, God has brought it about that it is their government; to be the government over a certain group of people is to be in a position of authority over them; and the people are to obey whatever those in a position of authority over them command them to do—unless they flagrantly order them to disobey some divine commandment.

Let's start with the first of these claims, that it is the God-given task of government to impose retributive punishment on wrongdoers. How is this interpretation arrived at? Well, in Romans 12:17–21, we read: "Repay no one evil for evil. . . . Never avenge yourselves, but leave it to the wrath of God; for it is written, 'Vengeance is mine, I will repay, says the Lord.' No, 'if your enemy is hungry, feed him; if he is thirsty, give him drink.' . . . Do not be overcome by evil, but overcome evil with good." Then in 13:4 we read: government "is the servant of God to execute . . . wrath on the wrongdoer."

The traditional interpretation of these passages goes as follows: we as individuals must not repay evil for evil; we must not avenge ourselves, not engage in retribution, not get even. Vengeance is God's business. But those who act in their position as government officials are not acting as private citizens; they are acting on God's behalf. When acting in their official position, it is their task to execute vengeance on behalf of God. Is this interpretation correct?

When Paul says that we must repay no one evil for evil, that we must instead overcome evil with good, he is repeating in his own words a central component of what Jesus said in the Sermon on the Mount. Matthew reports Jesus as saying, "You have heard that it was said, 'You shall love your neighbor and hate your enemy.' But I say to you, Love your enemies and pray for those who persecute you" (5:43–44). Luke reports him as saying, "Love your enemies, do good to those who hate you, bless those who curse you, pray for those who abuse you" (6:27–28).

Did Jesus have in mind an exception to what he said in his sermon? Was it his thought that though individual persons must live by the ethic of love, not repaying evil with evil but responding to evil with good, the state may live by a different rule? Was he allowing the state to repay evil with evil?

Nowhere does Jesus even hint at such an exception. Those who hold that he should be understood as having such an exception in mind bear the burden of proof, as do those who hold that Paul had such an exception in mind.

Ekdikēsis is the Greek word Paul uses in chapter 12 that gets translated in our English Bibles as "vengeance." If there is to be *ekdikēsis*, Paul says, it's God's business, not ours. Leave it to God. Paul directly connects *ekdikēsis* with "repaying."

The word *ekdikēsis* occurs nowhere in chapter 13. In 13:4 Paul does say that the ruler "is a servant of God, an *ekdikos* who executes wrath on the wrongdoer." My *Greek-English Lexicon of the New Testament* gives, as the meaning of *ekdikos*, "an avenger or one who punishes."[1] The former of these two possibilities would be compelling as the translation if Paul connected being an *ekdikos* with repaying. But nowhere in chapter 13 does he use the language of "repaying." He does not say that it is the business of government to repay evil with evil. What he does say is that rulers are "a terror" to bad conduct (v. 3) and that they are to "execute . . . wrath on the wrongdoer" (v. 4). Neither does he anywhere say that rulers act *on behalf of* God. He describes them as *servants* and *ministers* of God, not as deputies of God. I submit that the traditional interpretation is a misinterpretation.[2] The ruler is not an avenger but simply one who punishes.

---

1. Translated from the German of Walter Bauer by William F. Arndt and F. Wilbur Gingrich (Chicago: University of Chicago Press, 1974).

2. Romans 13:4 is usually translated to say that it is the ruler's task to execute *God's* wrath on wrongdoers. The Greek text speaks simply of wrath, not of God's wrath. If it had spoken of God's wrath, that would be a reason to interpret Paul as holding that the state acts on God's behalf.

I imagine an objection along the following lines. The distinction between *avenger* and *one who punishes* comes to nothing. Punishment is simply retribution; it is repaying evil with evil; it is vengeance. One who punishes is an avenger; an avenger is one who punishes. Not so. To see why not, let's reflect a bit on the nature of punishment.

What is punishment? Let me begin with a very general description: punishment is the imposition of hard treatment on someone because they did something wrong. I doubt that anyone would disagree with this description. What is the case, however, is that punishment, so understood, is often confused with other things in the region.

Notice that punishment, so understood, is intrinsically backward looking: somebody *did* something wrong and is *now* being punished *for* that *past* act. But hard treatment is often imposed on people for forward-looking reasons rather than for the backward-looking reason of their having done something wrong; it's imposed in the hope or expectation that it will bring about some good in the future. Hard treatment is sometimes imposed on someone in the hope or expectation of deterring other people from doing what he did. It is sometimes imposed on someone in the hope or expectation of reforming him so that he does not repeat what he did. And certain kinds of hard treatment—incarceration or exile—are sometimes imposed on someone so as to protect society from his repeating what he did.

Hard treatment imposed for any of these reasons—deterrence, reform, or security—is forward-looking. Rather than being imposed on someone *for* what he did in the past, it's imposed so as to secure some good in the future. Imposing hard treatment for any of these forward-looking reasons is not, strictly speaking, punishment. Punishment, to say it again, is the imposition of hard treatment on someone *for the wrong he did in the past*. Of course one can combine a backward-looking reason for imposing hard treatment with a forward-looking reason.

The definition of "punishment" that I gave is noncontroversial. The controversies surrounding punishment are not over its nature but over its rationale. Why impose hard treatment on someone for the wrong he did? What's the point of doing such a thing?

Far and away the most common answer to this question is the *retributive* theory of punishment. The basic idea is the following. My having wronged you created an imbalance of goods and evils in our engagement with each other. The goods are all on my side—or so I think; the harms or evils are all on your side. Retribution consists of redressing this imbalance. It consists, in more colloquial terminology, of paying back, of getting even. The point of punishment, says the retributivist, is to redress the imbalance of goods and evils that the wrong action created.

I quoted what Jesus said in his Sermon on the Mount: "Love your enemies and pray for those who persecute you." "Love your enemies, do good to those who hate you." Paul says the same thing: "Repay no one evil for evil." I see no way of interpreting what Jesus and Paul say other than as a rejection of retributive punishment. Retribution consists of repaying evil with evil, redressing harm with harm. Jesus and Paul reject retribution.

If retribution is out, is punishment out? It is not. Retribution is one way of understanding and practicing punishment; but it is not the only way. Consider the parent's punishment of his or her child. Unless the relationship of the parent to the child is seriously disordered, the parent does not think of this as paying back, does not think of this as redressing harm with harm, does not think of this as retribution. The parent understands what he or she is doing as reproving the child for what the child did, emphatically expressing condemnation of what the child did—usually with the hope that this will have a reforming effect on the child's future behavior. Let me invent the word *reprobative*, from *reprove*, and call this the *reprobative* account of punishment.

In our discussion of the relation between justice and love, we looked at some of the context of the second love command as it occurs in Leviticus 19:18. The verse immediately preceding the love command reads, "you shall reprove your neighbor, or you will incur guilt yourself" (NRSV). The idea is that we owe it to the neighbor, and perhaps to others as well, to reprove the neighbor if he or she does wrong; if we do not, we ourselves do wrong.

Now let's look once again at Paul's description of the task of the state. Let me quote the entire passage this time:

> Rulers are not a terror to good conduct, but to bad. Would you have no fear of him who is in authority? Then do what is good, and you will receive his approval, for he is God's servant for your good. But if you do wrong, be afraid, for he does not bear the sword in vain; he is the servant of God to execute wrath on the wrongdoer. (Rom. 13:3–4)

I submit that everything Paul says here fits the reprobative account of punishment. The state is not authorized to exercise retribution. The state is authorized, as are you and I, to exercise reprobative punishment.

What difference would it make if we think of the punishment exercised by the state as properly reprobative in nature rather than retributive? I don't know. I have not yet had time to think about this.

I think we can infer, from the social benefits that Paul cites of government carrying out its God-given assignment, that we would interpret him in too pinched and literalistic a fashion if we held that it was *only* punishment, strictly speaking, that he had in mind. The two main benefits Paul cites are being a terror (fear) to bad conduct and signaling support for good conduct. Paul's thought, so I suggest, is that God has assigned government the task not just of *punishing* wrongdoing once it has occurred but of *deterring* its occurrence and of *protecting* the public from its occurrence.

Government does this by publishing a law code that specifies actions that it forbids and to whose violation it attaches coercive sanctions; by establishing a judiciary to determine whether someone has violated the law and, if it determines that one has, to decree a punishment; and by setting up a police force to prevent or deter violations of the law. It is this whole threefold system that brings about the social benefits Paul cites of executing anger on wrongdoers—namely, making those who are contemplating doing wrong fearful of doing so and signaling support for those who do good. Paul's words "execute wrath on the wrongdoer" should be understood as a synecdoche for that more comprehensive task. The God-assigned task of government is to exercise governance over the public for the purpose of *curbing injustice* and *encouraging justice*. Of course government cannot curb all wrongdoing; it lacks the resources. To insult someone is to wrong that person; no government has the resources to curb all insults. Government has to set priorities, overlooking minor forms of wrongdoing and focusing on the serious.

What types of injustice is government commissioned by God to curb? Paul doesn't say. He knows nothing of our distinction between economic injustice and political injustice, nothing of our distinction between economic rights and political rights. If he had known of the distinction, he would have regarded it as irrelevant. What he would have learned from his study of "the law and the prophets" was that the king, when carrying out his assignment to establish justice in the land, was to give priority to the vulnerable and the downtrodden: the widows, the orphans, the aliens, and the impoverished. These are the ones for whom injustice is not an occasional episode but a daily condition; that's why they have priority. If there are people in society who are deprived of fair access to medical care or to adequate means of sustenance, then it is the God-assigned task of government to right this injustice. Exactly how government can best right some injustice depends on circumstances; different means fit different situations. But government does not have the option of ignoring the unjust condition of those at the bottom of the ladder of social power.

❖ 27 ❖

What Paul Said about
the Task and Authority
of the State

I mentioned that the traditional interpretation of the last five verses of Romans 12 and the first seven verses of Romans 13 has two main components. We have discussed one component, the claim that the God-given task of government is to impose retributive punishment on wrongdoers. What remains is to consider the other component.

The opening two verses of Romans 13 are the basis for this component of the traditional interpretation. It reads as follows in the NRSV translation: "Let every person be subject to the governing authorities; for there is no authority except from God, and those authorities that exist have been instituted by God. Therefore whoever resists authority resists what God has appointed, and those who resist will incur judgment." This has been interpreted as making or implying the following three claims: (1) whatever be the government of a certain group of people, God has brought it about that it is their government; (2) to be the government of a certain group of people is to be in a position of authority over them; and (3) the people are to do whatever those in a position of authority over them command them to do. The last of these claims was always interpreted as having an implicit qualification: unless those in authority flagrantly command them to disobey some divine command.

It is the belief that this is Paul's teaching concerning governmental authority, and concerning our proper response to such authority, that has led so many Christians over the centuries to passivity in the face of governmental injustice. A common charge by those Afrikaners who defended apartheid against the protesters was that they were disobeying God's command to obey the government.

I suggest that to understand Paul's teaching concerning governmental authority, we must read the first seven verses as a unit, not just the first two verses by themselves. Here are those first seven verses in the NRSV:

> Let every person be subject to the governing authorities [*exousiai*]; for there is no authority except from God, and those authorities that exist have been instituted [*tetagmenai*] by God. Therefore whoever resists authority resists what God has appointed, and those who resist will incur judgment [*krima*]. For rulers are not a terror [*phobos*] to good conduct, but to bad. Do you wish to have no fear [verbal form of *phobos*] of the authority? Then do what is good, and you will receive its approval; for it is God's servant [*diakonos*] for your good. But if you do what is wrong, you should be afraid, for the authority does not bear the sword in vain! It is the servant [*diakonos*] of God to execute wrath [*orgē*] on the wrongdoer. Therefore one must be subject, not only because of wrath but also because of conscience. For the same reason you also pay taxes, for the authorities are God's servants [*leitourgoi*] busy with this very thing. Pay to all what is due them—taxes to whom taxes are due, revenue to whom revenue is due, respect to whom respect is due, honor to whom honor is due.

To explain what I think is the main issue of interpretation here, let me introduce a distinction between two concepts of authority. One of these I call the concept of *performance authority*. Performance authority consists of the moral authority to do something—to issue commands, to declare a couple man and wife, to move into the White House, and so forth. To say that someone has the moral authority to do something is to imply that the person is morally permitted to do it; one cannot have the moral authority to do something that one is not morally permitted to do.

The other concept can appropriately be called the concept of *positional* or *institutional authority*. To possess positional or institutional authority is to *be in a position of authority*—that is, to occupy an institutional position that authorizes one to do certain things, including issuing directives to others. What comes along with possessing positional or institutional authority is always a certain jurisdiction. By virtue of being in that position of authority one is authorized to issue directives to certain people on certain matters—not to other people, and not to these people on other matters. If one is in an institutional position of authority and the directive that one issues falls within one's jurisdiction, then one has positional authority to issue it—even if, morally speaking, one ought not to have issued it. The fact that, morally speaking, one ought not to have issued it does not imply that it falls outside the jurisdiction of one's authority.

The traditional interpretation of the first two verses of Romans 13 employs the *institutional* or *positional* concept of authority. Let me once again present that interpretation: whatever be the government of a certain group of people, God has brought it about that it is their government; to be the government of a certain group of people is to be in a position of authority over them; and the people are to do whatever those in a position of authority over them command them to do—unless those in authority flagrantly command them to disobey some divine command.

Having interpreted the first two verses in this way, the traditional interpretation then interprets verses 3–5 as dealing not with the topic of authority but with the different, albeit related, topic of what those in positions of governmental authority *ought to do*.

I submit that the center of interpretation should not be verses 1–2 but verses 3–5, and that Paul should not be interpreted, in these verses, as leaving behind the topic of governmental authority but instead as telling what constitutes governmental authority. Government is a servant of God. As a servant of God it has a God-assigned task to perform. Its God-assigned task is to exercise governance over the public for the purpose of executing wrath or anger on wrongdoers, thereby indicating its approval of doing good. If God assigns it that task, then God both authorizes and enjoins it to perform that task. And if God authorizes it to perform that task, then it has the authority to do that, the God-given authority to exercise governance over the public for the purpose of executing wrath on wrongdoers and thereby indicating its approval of doing good. The concept of authority that Paul employs is not the concept of institutional authority but the concept of performance authority.

Because God has authorized and enjoined government to exercise governance over the public for the purpose of curbing injustice and encouraging justice, the people must submit, says Paul; they must obey, be subject, conform (the verb is *hypotassō*). Paul does not say here that they are to submit because government officials are "in a position of authority" or because they "have authority." They are to submit because God's purpose in appointing government to curb injustice and encourage justice would not be achieved if the people did not submit. In general, they are to render to the governmental authorities what is due them: taxes to whom taxes are due, respect to whom respect is due, honor to whom honor is due.

Paul says that they are to submit "not only because of wrath but also because of conscience [*syneidēsin*]." By "because of wrath" Paul surely means "out of fear of sanctions." Paul does not condemn submitting because one judges that one is likely to be punished if one does not. But what he emphasizes is that the people should submit out of conscience. Along with most commentators I interpret this as meaning that they are *morally obligated to submit*. The directives that the government issues to the public for the purpose of curbing injustice are binding.

But suppose that government itself becomes a wrongdoer. This can take at least four forms. The government may turn a blind eye to serious wrongdoing among the citizens and those living or traveling within its territory. It may issue directives to citizens and others that amount to commanding them to do wrong. It may itself directly wrong citizens and others by the directives it issues to them, denying them their right to religious freedom, their right to assemble, and so forth. Or it may itself directly wrong citizens and foreigners by the sort of force and coercion it applies to them.

If God commissions government to exercise governance over the public for the purpose of executing wrath on wrongdoers, then obviously God does not authorize government itself to become a wrongdoer in any of these ways. All such actions fall outside the divine authorization. We can say something stronger. Not only does God's authorization not extend to authorizing the state itself to become a wrongdoer, God does not *permit* the government to issue directives or employ forms of coercion that constitute wrongdoing on the part of the government. What sense would it make for God to commission government to exercise governance over the public for the purpose of executing anger against individual wrongdoers while permitting government itself to be a wrongdoer?

Paul neither says nor suggests that if officials in a position of authority order the members of the public to do something, and that order falls within the jurisdiction of their institutional authority, then that order generates in the public the obligation to obey. He neither says nor suggests this for the reason that he is not working with the concept of institutional authority. He's working with the concept of performance authority—more specifically, with the concept of authority to govern. God commissions government to do something—namely, to exercise governance over the public with the aim of curbing injustice. If the state is not morally permitted to issue a certain directive to the public, then, should it nonetheless do so, its doing so generates in the public no obligation to obey. The fact that it was issued by officials in a position of authority, and that it falls within the scope of their institutional authority, makes no difference. There may be good prudential reasons for obeying anyway, but the directive has not generated in the people the obligation to obey.

Let us now turn to the two opening verses of Romans 13. I suggest that Paul is saying substantially the same thing in these first two verses as what he says, in a more amplified way, in verses 3–5; it's because of the amplification that we should take 3–5 as the center of our interpretation and interpret verses 1–2 in their light, rather than the other way around. "Let every person be subject to the governing authorities," says Paul. The verb translated here as "subject" is the same as the one translated in verse 5 as "subject"—namely, *hypotassō*. Why should everybody be subject to the governing authorities? Because "those authorities that exist have been instituted by God." With verse 4 in mind, our immediate thought is that they are not just instituted, *period, full stop*. That's how the passage has traditionally been read, with interpreters tossing off suggestions as to what Paul might mean by saying that God "institutes" governing authorities. But from verse 4 we know that they are instituted *to do* something, appointed to *do* something, and we know what that is: to curb injustice.

When the sentence is thus understood as elliptical, "instituted" proves a rather poor translation of the verb *hypotassō*; better is the first meaning that my Greek-English lexicon gives for the verb, "appointed." They are *appointed*, appointed *to do* something; "appointed" is the translation that the NRSV gives for the word *diatagē* in verse 2. Governing authorities are appointed by God to exercise governance over the public for the purpose of executing anger on wrongdoers, and in that way to serve God. They are commissioned by God to do this, assigned to do this, thereby authorized and enjoined to do this. And so it is that when they do what they are assigned to do, we must not resist them but obey and submit; to resist them would be to resist their doing what God has assigned them to do, authorized and enjoined them to do. This is how the argument gets fleshed out in verses 3–5. In verses 1 and 2 the full argument is alluded to but not fleshed out.

The traditional interpretation of Paul's declaration, that "those authorities that exist have been instituted by God," is that whoever is in a position of authority has been placed in that position by God. But if we agree that verses 3–5 flesh out Paul's thought in the two opening verses, then that is an exceedingly implausible interpretation—completely ad hoc, unrelated to the main argument. Paul is not saying that whoever occupies some governmental position of authority does so because God has put the person in that position; he is saying that whoever finds oneself in such a position, however that came about, has a commission from God, an assignment, to serve God by exercising governance over the public for the purpose of executing anger on wrongdoers.

Last, what about that other clause in verse 1, "there is no authority except from God"? I think it highly unlikely that Paul is here inserting into his argument an abstract comment about authority in general; possible, but not likely. He's talking about the authority of what he calls "governing authorities." What Paul is saying is that resisting the government, when the government is carrying out its God-assigned task, is never merely resisting the government but always resisting something else as well. That something else is God—not some Roman deity, not one of those transcendent authorities or powers of which Paul speaks in other places. Government authorities have been assigned by God to deter, prevent, and punish wrongdoing. No heavenly being other than God has assigned them to do this.

To summarize: it is the God-given task of government to curb injustice in society and thereby to secure justice. It does this by establishing a just system of laws, a just and effective police force, and a just judiciary.

The picture of political authority and obedience that Paul presented to the Roman Christians was not an innovation on his part; it was the same as that which dominates the Old Testament. The central task of the ruler is to secure justice. In Psalm 72 we get a classic presentation. I quote from the Jerusalem Bible:

> God, give your own justice to the king,
>   your own [doing what is right][1] to the royal son,
> so that he may rule your people rightly
>   and your poor with justice.
> Let the mountains and hills
>   bring a message of peace [shalom] for the people.
> Uprightly he will defend the poorest,
> he will save the children of those in need,
>   and crush their oppressors. (vv. 1–4)

It will now be clear why I said earlier that the Honduran organization Association for a More Just Society implicitly operates with a profoundly Pauline understanding of the task and authority of government. The Association does not teach passivity in the face of the failure by Honduran officials to curb injustice and secure justice in Honduras. It does not content itself with giving aid to the victims of injustice. But neither does it try to do an end run around government. It insists that the Honduran government do what God has authorized it to do—namely, to curb injustice and thereby secure justice—and it aids and assists the government in carrying out that task.

At a certain point in the resistance movement in South Africa, its leaders organized a prayer service for the purpose of praying to God for the downfall of the state (I will say more about this in the final chapter). This evoked an enormous negative reaction. It was said to be theologically heretical to pray for the downfall of the government that God had put in place.

I submit that, to the contrary, the leaders had a profoundly Pauline understanding of governmental authority. The government of South Africa was authorized by God to curb injustice and thereby to secure justice. It was flagrantly failing to do what God had authorized it to do. In that situation, believers pray to God that it do what it is authorized to do. If it adamantly refuses, they pray for its downfall.

---

1. For "doing what is right" the Jerusalem Bible has "righteousness."

❖ 28 ❖

Justice, Forgiveness, and Punishment

We who are Christians cannot discuss primary justice without discussing the relation of such justice to the love for one's neighbor that Jesus enjoins on us; and we cannot discuss reactive justice in general, or punishment in particular, without considering how forgiveness is related to reactive justice and to punishment.

The two topics, justice and love, and justice and forgiveness, are of course connected. Forgiveness is a manifestation of the love that Scripture attributes to God and that Jesus enjoins on us. Anders Nygren went further and held that we should think of all love on the model of God's forgiveness of the sinner. That goes too far. But there can be no doubt that love manifested in forgiveness is a fundamental component of the Christian vision.

Anyone who has read around in the twentieth-century philosophical and theological literature on forgiveness will have discovered that there is no consensus on the nature of forgiveness. So let me briefly explain what I take forgiveness to be, without, on this occasion, arguing against alternative views.

Everyone would agree that forgiveness cannot be dispensed indiscriminately hither and yon. Forgiveness presupposes that someone has wronged someone, deprived the person of something to which the person had a right; it presupposes that an injustice has occurred. It furthermore presupposes that the one doing the forgiving *recognizes* that someone has been wronged, *recognizes* that an injustice has occurred.

Let me now present my understanding of the nature of forgiveness in two stages. First I will describe the context required if forgiveness is to occur. Then I will say what forgiveness does within that context. Let me introduce a fictional character and call him "Hubert."

The context in which my forgiveness of Hubert can occur has five essential components: (1) Hubert did wrong me, (2) I rightly believe that he was blamable for doing so, (3) I feel resentment or some similar negative emotion at the deed done, (4) I feel anger or some similar negative emotion at Hubert for having done it, and (5) I continue to remember the deed and who did it, and continue to condemn it. Only when these conditions are met is it possible for me to forgive Hubert for the wrong he did me.

I said that everyone would agree that the first of these is a necessary condition of my forgiving Hubert. Let me briefly explain why the others are as well.

I can forgive Hubert for his wronging of me only if I rightly believe that he was blamable, culpable, for what he did. If I believe that he was not culpable because he acted under duress, out of nonculpable ignorance, or out of ineradicable weakness of will, I do not blame him and hence do not forgive him. I excuse him. Excusing resembles forgiving, but it is nonetheless not only distinct from forgiving but also forestalls forgiving. If I excuse you, forgiveness is out of the picture.

Second, it's possible to believe that one has been wronged by someone without experiencing any negative emotion toward either deed or doer. One might dismiss act and agent as beneath one's attention. "I can't be bothered with insults from scum like you." Such emotionless dismissal is not forgiveness; it too forestalls forgiveness. It does not treat the deed and its doer with moral seriousness. Forgiveness can occur only when the deed and its doer are treated with moral seriousness.

Third, if I am to forgive Hubert for the wrong he did me, I must continue to remember what was done to me, I must continue to remember that it was Hubert who did it, and I must continue to condemn what he did. Forgetting what was done to me, or forgetting that Hubert did it, whether because I actively put the memory out of mind or because it just gradually fades away, resembles forgiveness. But forgetting is not forgiving; it too forestalls forgiving. If one has forgotten what was done to one or forgotten who did it, forgiving the person for what the person did is out of the picture. Forgiveness is not to be identified with letting bygones be bygones.

So what is it to forgive Hubert for the wrong he did me? I suggest that it is to enact the resolution no longer to hold against him what he did to me, no longer to count it against him. My full enactment of the resolution may take a long time; it may, in fact, never be completed. Forgiveness is often hard work. And the resolution itself may be partial: I may resolve not to hold it against him in some ways and resolve to continue to hold it against him in other ways.

And what is it for me no longer to hold against Hubert what he did to me, no longer to count it against him? He did it after all, I remember that he did, and I continue to condemn it; I have neither forgotten what he did nor have I excused him for doing it.

To explain what I think it is, let me distinguish between what I will call a person's *personal* history and what I will call his (or her) *moral* history. Someone's personal history is the ensemble of all the things he did. His moral history is a subset within his personal history. It consists of that ensemble of things he did that contribute to determining in what respects and to what degree he is a morally good person, and in what respects and to what degree he is morally bad.

The point of introducing the idea of a person's moral history is that we need not, and do not, treat everything a person does as part of his moral history. If Hubert wronged me but it turns out that he's not morally blamable because he acted out of nonculpable ignorance, then, rather than thinking worse of him for what he did to me, I excuse him. To excuse him is to declare that the deed is not part of his moral history. It is part of his personal history; he did do it. But it's not part of his *moral* history; it does not put a blot on his moral condition.

I suggest that for me not to hold against Hubert the wrong he did to me is for me, in my personal engagement with him, to treat him as if that deed did not belong to his moral history. It is in fact part of his moral history, and I don't forget that it is; I both remember what he did and continue to condemn it. But I now act on the resolution to treat him as I would if I did not believe that it was part of his moral history. I treat him as I would if I excused him—except that I continue to believe that he is blamable.

Assuming that this is what forgiveness is, why forgive? Why not continue to hold against Hubert the wrong he did to me? Why not resolve that the dastardly thing he did shall forever determine how I interact with him?

Well, suppose that Hubert has repented of what he did to me. He remains culpable for having done it; nothing can change that. But he has altered his relation to what he did in a morally significant way. Rather than standing behind what he did to me, he now places himself at a moral distance from it. He now joins me in condemning what he did. His overall moral condition is now significantly different from what it was before. And not only different; in an important respect, better. Hubert's repentance, assuming I know about it, is an *invitation* for me to forgive him.

His repentance is no more than an invitation, however; my forgiveness may not be forthcoming. As we all know, some people reject the invitation that repentance offers. They refuse to forgive the wrongdoer, even if he has repented of what he did and they know he has.

Suppose, however, that I accept the invitation that Hubert's repentance offers me. I forgive him. Presumably I do so because I expect or hope that thereby some good will come about. What might that good be?

Often we forgive the repentant wrongdoer in the hope or expectation that reconciliation will ensue. Reconciliation is the good that we expect or hope forgiveness in response to repentance will bring about.

Perhaps there is something more that we hope for, or should hope for. I have in mind a comment by the philosopher Jean Hampton. After observing that "[forgiveness] makes possible the benefits that come from a renewed relationship," she goes on to say the following:

> It also liberates [the victim and the wrongdoer] from the effects of the immoral action itself. The forgiver is no longer trapped in the position of the victim defending herself, and the wrongdoer is no longer in the position of the sinner, stained by sin and indebted to his victim. But perhaps the greatest good forgiveness can bring is the liberation of the wrongdoer from the effects of the victim's moral hatred. If the wrongdoer fears that the victim is right to see him as cloaked in evil, or as infected with moral sin, these fears can engender moral hatred of himself.[1]

These seem to me wise and perceptive words.

The explanation of forgiveness that I have offered is an explanation of what the theological and philosophical traditions call forgiveness. In the modern therapeutic tradition, something quite different is called forgiveness.

Forgiveness, as I have described it, is an *engagement* with the wrongdoer; one engages the person as if what the person did does not belong to his or her moral history. The pair, forgiveness and repentance together, is a two-way engagement. What is called forgiveness in the modern therapeutic tradition is not an engagement with the wrongdoer. It's the process of getting over one's emotions of anger at the wrongdoer and resentment at the deed done so that they no longer "eat away" at one—no longer impair one's well-being. Getting over these emotions is typically recommended on the ground that doing so

1. Jean Hampton, "Forgiveness, Resentment, and Hatred," in Jeffrie Murphy and Jean Hampton, *Forgiveness and Mercy* (Cambridge: Cambridge University Press, 1988), 86.

enables one to "get on with things"; it is also often recommended on the ground that unless one gets over one's anger and resentment, the wrongdoer continues to have emotional control over one. Both one's well-being and one's autonomy are enhanced by getting over one's anger. Forgiveness, so understood, is a purely interior undertaking. It does not aim at reconciliation between wrongdoer and victim; it aims at getting one's own emotional house in order. Sometimes, let me be clear, this is the best one can do; but it's a *second* best.

Back to what is called forgiveness in the theological and philosophical traditions. I described repentance as an *invitation* to forgive. A question that Christians often ask is whether they—and perhaps others as well—should forgive even in the absence of repentance. What Jesus said on the cross is commonly cited in support of the claim that we should. Referring to those who were crucifying him, Jesus said, "Father, forgive them; for they know not what they do" (Luke 23:34).

As I observed earlier, if someone wrongs somebody but doesn't know that she did (and couldn't be expected to have known), we don't blame her for what she did but excuse her. And if we excuse her rather than blame her, forgiveness is not in the picture. One can forgive someone for what she did only if one thinks she is blamable.

The Greek word that is translated into English as "forgive" in Luke 23:34 is an imperative form of the verb *aphiēmi*. My Greek-English lexicon tells me that the root meaning of the term is *let go, send away*. In some contexts the term does undoubtedly mean *forgive*. But given that Jesus says that his crucifiers don't know what they are doing, what he is asking of the Father is not that he forgive them but that he excuse them—not hold it against them.

Luke reports Jesus as saying, on one occasion, "If another disciple sins, you must rebuke the offender, and if there is repentance, you must forgive. And if the same person sins against you seven times a day, and turns back to you seven times and says, 'I repent,' you must forgive" (Luke 17:3–4 NRSV). In Matthew's narrative, Peter seems to have found this quite incredible. To check it out he asks, "Lord, if another member of the church sins against me, how often should I forgive?

As many as seven times?" Jesus's response is hyperbolic: "Not seven times, but, I tell you, seventy-seven times" (Matt. 18:21–22 NRSV).[2]

Nowhere in the New Testament is Jesus reported as enjoining his listeners to forgive unrepentant wrongdoers. We are instructed to love our enemies, including those who have wronged us and are unrepentant. We are not instructed to forgive our enemies. Neither do I know of any passage in the New Testament that says that God forgives (justifies) even unrepentant wrongdoers. Here is what the *Kairos Document*, issued in South Africa in 1986 by theologians opposed to apartheid, says on the matter:

> The Biblical teaching on reconciliation and forgiveness makes it quite clear that nobody can be forgiven and reconciled with God unless she or he repents of their sins. Nor are we expected to forgive the unrepentant sinner. When he or she repents we must be willing to forgive seventy times seven times but before that we are expected to preach repentance to those who sin against us or against anyone. Reconciliation, forgiveness and negotiations will become our Christian duty in South Africa only when the apartheid regime shows signs of genuine repentance.[3]

A further question is whether it is even *possible* to forgive the unrepentant wrongdoer—and if it is possible, whether it is morally *permissible*. Suppose that Hubert stands behind what he did to me; he insists that he did me no wrong. Can I nonetheless form and act on the resolution to forgive him, not hold it against him in my future engagements with him? I can certainly be *willing* to forgive him in case he repents. But can I forgive?

2. What immediately follows in Matthew's Gospel is Jesus's parable about the unforgiving servant: a king out of mercy forgave the very large debt of one of his slaves, whereupon this slave turned around and refused to forgive the minor debt to him of one of his fellow slaves. When the king heard about this, he was angry with the first slave, and ordered him to be punished. "Should you not have had mercy on your fellow slave," he said, "as I had mercy on you?" Jesus concludes the story with these words: "So my heavenly Father will also do to every one of you, if you do not forgive your brother or sister from your heart" (vv. 33, 35 NRSV).

3. *Kairos Document*, §3.1; online at http://www.sahistory.org.za/archive/challenge-church-theological-comment-political-crisis-south-africa-kairos-document-1985.

Possibly; I'm not sure. But I question whether I should. Not to hold it against him in the absence of any repentance on his part is to fail to take with full moral seriousness either the wrongness of the deed, my own worth, or Hubert's worth as a moral agent. Consider the situation. Hubert agrees with me that what he did should be counted as belonging to his moral history; but he insists, over my objections, that what he did was not wrong but was in fact a good thing. Now I say to him, "We agree that you are responsible for what you did to me; but you don't see anything wrong in it. I do. What you did to me was wrong. But I have resolved not to hold it against you. I forgive you. I have resolved henceforth to treat you as I would if I excused you." I submit that this is both to demean myself and to insult Hubert by refusing to treat him and what he did with full moral seriousness. "Keep your forgiveness," he snaps, "I did nothing wrong." Better to join with Hubert in counting the deed as part of his moral history and go on to insist, against his protests, that it was wrong.

Richard Swinburne makes the point well. Unless the wrongdoing was trivial, it is wrong for the victim "in the absence of some atonement at least in the form of apology to treat the [act] as not having been done."[4] If I have murdered your wife and you decide to overlook my offense and interact with me as if it had never happened, your attitude "trivializes human life, your love for your wife, and the importance of right action. And it involves your failing to treat me seriously, to take seriously my attitude towards you expressed in my action. Thereby it trivializes human relationships, for it supposes that good human relations can exist when we do not take each other seriously."[5]

Let me close with some reflections on the relation of forgiveness to punishment. Suppose that Hubert has repented of what he did to me, that I know that he has, and that I am working at forgiving him. Though I believe that Hubert has genuinely repented of this particular act, I might also believe that he still has "demons" inside

---

4. Richard Swinburne, *Responsibility and Atonement* (Oxford: Oxford University Press, 1989), 85–86.

5. Ibid., 86.

him that make it likely that he will do the same sort of thing again, if not to me, then to someone else. In that case I might support the imposition of hard treatment on him of a sort that is likely to reform him—treatment that is likely to induce in him a character reformation. I might also think that, until this reformation has taken place, the public needs to be protected from him. And I might think that if our system for deterring such behavior is to work, it has to be imposed impartially; it won't work effectively and fairly if we allow those who impress us with their penitence to avoid sanctions. In short, I might be convinced that hard treatment of the appropriate sort should be imposed on Hubert for reformation, for protection, or for deterrence.

But as I noted earlier, none of these reasons for imposing one or another sort of hard treatment on someone is punishment, strictly speaking. They all point forward to some good to be achieved in the future, whereas punishment looks back to some wrong that has been done. To punish is to impose hard treatment on someone for the *wrong* the person did *in the past*.

So suppose that Hubert is thoroughly penitent and that I forgive him. I act on the resolution not to hold against him what he did to me; I interact with him as if he had not done it. Do I then forego imposing or supporting the imposition of punishment on him—reprobative punishment? In reprobative punishment, the imposition of hard treatment *counts as* firmly condemning what was done.

If I no longer hold against Hubert what he did to me, if I fully and completely forgive him, then I will not myself impose hard treatment on him as a way of firmly condemning him for what he did, nor will I be in favor of the state or any other institution doing so. To condemn him in this way, or to support his being condemned, amounts to counting against him what he did.

This raises the question, however, whether there may not be some cases in which it would be inappropriate, perhaps even wrong, to forego punishment of the wrongdoer even if he is penitent—inappropriate or wrong to forego firmly expressing condemnation of what he did. Yes, he now joins me in condemning what he did. But may it be that what he did was so bad that verbal condemnation is inadequate? May it be that some stronger form of condemnation is needed?

I think so. In many ways, one will forgive him. But one will not think it right to forego punishing him nor to forego supporting his being punished. One's forgiveness, in that way, does and should remain incomplete.

PART 6

BEAUTY, HOPE, AND JUSTICE

❖ 29 ❖

Justice and Beauty

I often recall the image of those gorgeous hills in Kenya trying to regurgitate that sordid mission compound that had been forced down their throat. Was there perhaps some deep connection between my response to this ugliness and my response to the cry for the righting of injustice that I subsequently heard at the conference in Potchefstroom? Is ugliness connected somehow to injustice? Conversely, is beauty, or aesthetic goodness, connected somehow to justice?

I mentioned earlier that on the flight back from Potchefstroom, the worry came over me that my life was becoming irreparably fractured. I loved philosophy; I had come to care deeply about liturgy; I loved the arts. Speaking up for these wronged people had now been added to my agenda. Was there anything that united these loves, anything that held them together? Or did I have to be content with living a fractured life? I noted that some time later it occurred to me that what unites love of understanding, worship, beauty, and justice is that these are all dimensions of shalom. In shalom, understanding has replaced bewilderment, worship of God has replaced enmity, aesthetic delight has replaced revulsion, justice has replaced injustice.

I want now to go further, and explore the possibility of one or two yet deeper connections between justice and beauty. In the spring of 2007, the well-known American poet Donald Hall visited the University of Virginia. He read his poetry to a large audience and led a small seminar for students on writing poetry. Though I was neither a student nor a poet, I was invited to be a hanger-on in the seminar.

In the seminar, Hall every now and then illustrated the point he wanted to make by pointing to changes he had made in one of his own poems from earlier drafts to the final version. I remember one change he said he had made. In a draft of one of his poems he had spoken of a dog as wagging its tail; in the final version he spoke of the dog as *swinging* its tail. A student asked him why he made the change. Hall's answer was that it made it a better poem. He didn't explain why it made it a better poem, nor did anyone ask him why; I think we all just felt, *of course*.

I was probably the only person in the room sufficiently struck by this remark to remember it. Let me explain why it struck me. The standard view in present-day philosophy of art as to the worth of a work of the arts is that its worth is located in the aesthetic pleasure it gives to those who listen to it, read it, or look at it. The assumption is that aesthetically pleasurable experiences are *intrinsically* worthwhile, and that works of art are a means to the end of producing such intrinsically worthwhile experiences. That's what makes them good. Their worth is instrumental. Their worth is like the worth of a tool. A tool is something that one uses as a means to accomplish something. It's what one accomplishes with the tool that is the intrinsically worthwhile thing; the tool is just a means to that. Hammers are not of intrinsic worth. What makes a hammer good is that it is good *for* pounding nails. Works of art are like tools in this respect. What makes them good is that they produce something that we regard as valuable, in this case, pleasurable experiences. That's the dominant idea.

Now return to what Hall said. He did not say that he made the change because he thought his readers would get greater pleasure from having a dog described as swinging its tail than from having it described as wagging its tail. Audience pleasure is, in general, a highly unpredictable thing. But neither did he identify any other effect that he was trying to bring about. He said that he made the change because it made it a better poem. He was assuming that poems have intrinsic worth. He was assuming that some poems are *intrinsically* better poems than others. Whether poems are a means to some kind of experience—pleasure or whatever—was not in view.

I think Hall was right about this. Works of art do have intrinsic worth. At least part of what is worthwhile about looking at them, listening to them, and reading them is that thereby one becomes aware of this thing of worth and of that in it which gives it worth. The poem does not get its basic worth from the fact that reading it causes a pleasurable experience. It's the other way around: what makes it worth reading is that thereby one becomes perceptually aware of something of worth.

In his comment, Hall was reflecting the traditional understanding of beauty. Beauty, said Aquinas, is that which pleases when seen. What he had in mind is this: reality is filled with things that resemble God in that they are good or excellent—excellent philosophy papers, excellent sunsets, excellent persons, excellent colleges and universities, and so forth, on and on. Some of these things of worth or excellence are such that we experience sensory delight in attending to them. Those are the things that we describe as beautiful. They are not excellent *because* they effect in us a certain experience, that of sensory delight. Their excellence is out there, as it were, intrinsic to them. But it's a different kind of excellence from that of, say, a college or university. What's distinctive about it is that one experiences sensory delight in attending to it.

Now recall the theory of justice that I developed. I said that justice characterizes our social relationships insofar as we are treated as we have a right to be treated; and I said that to be treated as one has a right to be treated is to be treated in a way that befits one's worth.

A deep connection between aesthetic joy and acting justly is now right before us. Persons and human beings have worth; to treat them justly is to treat them as befits their worth. Things available to our hearing, our seeing, and our reading also have worth; aesthetic joy or delight is the delight one experiences in attending to these things and taking note of their worth. The injustice of apartheid was a violation of worth; the ugliness of the mission compound was a repudiation of worth.

Let me close with a question. Is there perhaps a yet tighter connection between injustice and ugliness? May it be that, sometimes at least, ugliness is a form of injustice? May it be that, sometimes at least, a person is being wronged by being forced to live, or left to live, in aesthetically squalid surroundings that give no sensory delight?

Let it be agreed that shalom includes sensory delight. My question is not whether the love that seeks shalom for one's fellow human beings will seek for them surroundings in which they can find sensory delight. Of course it will. My question is whether we are violating the dignity of our fellow human beings when we force them to live in aesthetically squalid surroundings, or when we rest content with letting them live in such surroundings.

The Inner City Christian Federation (ICCF) is based in Grand Rapids, Michigan, and works there in the inner city. It sees itself as a justice organization. In its mission statement it declares, "In response to God's call to justice, the Inner City Christian Federation provides housing opportunities and services that encourage family responsibility and independence, thereby helping to build stable communities."

ICCF rejects the all-too-common practice of razing sections of the inner city and erecting apartment buildings on the razed ground. Instead it buys houses and renovates them; and it buys empty lots and houses that have fallen into hopeless disrepair and hires architects to design individual houses and duplexes that fit stylistically into the neighborhood. Though the houses it designs and builds are simple, ICCF does not build as cheaply as possible; it uses quality materials that will last. As of this writing, ICCF has built or renovated almost six hundred dwellings.

ICCF is sensitive to good color choices, attractive landscaping, and spacious fenestration. An important component of the program it gives to the architects who design for it is that the houses be beautiful, or as it often prefers to say, that they show good design. Here is its statement of its core values:

> Through all of ICCF's financial, construction and enablement activities three core values are present:
>
> **Respect**: Created in the image of God, our residents are very special people. In all of our contacts, we treat them with respect. One way of doing so is to *expect* from them responsibility and a commitment to personal growth.
>
> **Opportunity**: Our residents are met "where they are" and then have the opportunity to press toward a greater housing goal.
>
> **Beauty**: Beauty is a gift of God. It serves to enrich our lives and help instill pride and dignity. All of ICCF's houses are designed to be beautiful and blend harmoniously with surrounding structures.

In a personal communication, a spokesperson for ICCF wrote the following about its headquarters building: "The value ICCF places on beauty is also affirmed in our offices on 920 Cherry Street. This century-old building with Greek revival architecture by a well-known Chicago architect and its gorgeous gardens tell our clients who come here for services, 'We value you. You deserve a beautiful place to come to for classes and counseling.'"

It's easy for those involved in service organizations to fall into the trap of assuming that to be a human being is to be a food-eater, a clothes-wearer, and a house-dweller; more often than not the people one is dealing with don't have enough food to eat and don't have adequate clothes to wear; more often than not their housing is squalid or nonexistent. Food, clothing, and housing are urgent. Justice requires that one give priority to those.

But to be human is more, much more, than this. To be human is to be a creature who is treated with disrespect if she is deprived of education. To be human is to be a creature who is treated with disrespect if she is not allowed, to a considerable extent, to set her own course of life rather than have someone else set it for her. And to be human is to be a creature who is treated with disrespect if she is forced to live in aesthetic squalor. When social arrangements force some of our fellow human beings to live in poverty, those human beings are wronged, treated unjustly. But it's also true that when social arrangements force some of our fellow human beings to live in aesthetic squalor, those human beings are wronged, treated unjustly. We demean our fellow human beings when we force them to live in surroundings that cannot possibly give any sensory refreshment, or when we rest content with letting them live in such surroundings. The opportunity to live in surroundings of aesthetic decency is not an optional luxury. Justice requires it.

❖ 30 ❖

Hope

It's easy to feel overwhelmed by the injustices of the world. So many causes beg for attention that one becomes immobilized. To those who feel immobilized I say: support whatever be the cause to which you bear some special relation. It may be a cause that's close to home; it may be a cause that's far away. Through little of my own doing I came to bear a special relation to the cause of ending apartheid in South Africa, to the ongoing cause of the Palestinians, and to ASJ's cause of justice in Honduras. If you happen not to bear any special relation to any cause, just pick one that does good and important work and that needs support.

An ever-present menace to those who are working in some cause to right injustice is *burnout*. The cause seems to be getting nowhere; one loses hope. In this penultimate chapter I want to reflect on the sort of hope that the struggle for the righting of injustice requires—both the righting of primary injustice, which is what the anti-apartheid movement was struggling for in South Africa, and for the righting of reactive injustice, which is what the Honduran organization ASJ is struggling for.

Every human endeavor that is not coerced requires, as a minimum, the hope that its goal will be achieved. Optimism is not required—optimism being understood as the expectation that one will achieve what one endeavors. The ambulance attendant who endeavors to resuscitate the person pulled down by the waves may not expect to succeed in his endeavor; he may not be at all optimistic. Yet as long as there is hope, he tries. Once he gives up hope, he stops trying.

To the principle that every endeavor requires hope there are a few exceptions. Sometimes one tries to do something to find out whether or not it's hopeless; the person in the emergency room asks you to try to move your arm to find out whether you can. And sometimes one tries to do something to prove that it's hopeless. But apart from such cases, endeavor presupposes hope—not optimism, but hope. Though let it be said that sometimes we give up on an endeavor if we are not optimistic about its success. It's just not worth trying.

Working for the righting of injustice does not require optimism; sometimes one works for the righting of injustice in situations like that of the ambulance attendant who tries to resuscitate his patient with no expectation one way or another as to whether he will succeed. What working for the righting of injustice does require is hope—hope of a peculiar sort, as we shall see. I should state here that what follows are *Christian* reflections on the sort of hope that the struggle for the righting of injustice requires.

Thomas Aquinas, in the first part of the second part of his *Summa theologiae*, offers a characteristically lucid analysis of hope. Hope, at bottom, is a special form of desire, says Aquinas. It is unlike fear in that its object is a *good* of some sort—or at least, something that the agent regards as good. It is unlike joy in that its object is a future rather than a present good. It is unlike the desire for small things in that, in Aquinas's words, its object is "something arduous and difficult to obtain." We do not "speak of any one hoping for trifles, which are in one's power to have at any time." And it is unlike despair in that "this difficult thing is something possible to obtain: for one does not hope for that which one cannot get at all."[1] An admirable analysis, I say!

Later in the same part of his *Summa*, Aquinas asks whether hope, along with faith and charity, is to be regarded as one of the theological virtues or whether it is an intellectual or moral virtue. First he explains the difference: "The object of the theological virtues is God Himself, Who is the last end of all, as surpassing the knowledge of our reason. On the other hand, the object of the intellectual and moral virtues is something comprehensible to human reason."[2]

Aquinas argues that faith, hope, and charity are theological virtues. His argument goes like this. For human beings there is the possibility of "supernatural happiness," this consisting in a delighted knowledge of God that goes beyond what can be achieved by the use of our ordinary human capacities. If we human beings are to achieve supernatural happiness, we need some sort of supplement to our creaturely capacities—some sort of "supernatural" addition. Aquinas takes faith, hope, and charity to be the results of such an addition.

What I want to take from this quick dip into the deep waters of Aquinas's *Summa theologiae* is his claim that Christian hope is hope for consummation—consummation here being understood as a supernatural mode of union with God. Christian hope, as Aquinas understands it, is not hope for what might transpire in history. Hence it has nothing in particular to do with the struggle for the righting of injustice in this world of ours. Christian hope is not hope that our struggle for the righting of injustice will bear fruit, nor is it hope that our longing for the righting of injustice will be satisfied; it is hope for a state of happiness that transcends history. It is my impression that, in understanding Christian hope in this way, Aquinas is representative of a long and prominent strand of Christian thought.

I judge it to be a theological mistake to confine Christian hope to hope for consummation. Recall the story of the numinous burning

1. Question 40, article 1 (*resp.*); online at http://www.newadvent.org/summa/2040 .htm.
2. Question 62, article 2 (*resp.*); online at http://www.newadvent.org/summa/2062 .htm.

bush in Exodus 3. The curiosity of Moses, the fugitive shepherd, was piqued one day by a flaming bush that was not burned up. He went to investigate. As he approached, he heard, from the region of the bush, the sound of a voice addressing him by name and telling him to keep his distance and take off his shoes, for he was on holy ground. The speaker then identified himself—what Moses heard was indeed the speech of a speaker, not just voices haunting a disturbed mind. "I am the God of your father, the God of Abraham, the God of Isaac, and the God of Jacob" (v. 6), said the speaker. Having thus identified himself, God went on to say, "I have seen the affliction of my people who are in Egypt, and have heard their cry because of their taskmasters; I know their sufferings, and I have come down to deliver them out of the hand of the Egyptians, and to bring them up out of that land to a good and broad land, a land flowing with milk and honey" (vv. 7–8).

Now jump to the song (in the first chapter of Luke) that the elderly Zechariah was moved to sing upon the birth of his son, John, the one known to us as John the Baptist:

> Blessed be the Lord God of Israel,
> for he has visited and redeemed his people,
> and has raised up a horn of salvation for us
> in the house of his servant David,
> as he spoke by the mouth of his holy prophets from of old,
> that we should be saved from our enemies,
> and from the hand of all who hate us;
> to perform the mercy promised to our fathers,
> and to remember his holy covenant,
> the oath which he swore to our father Abraham, to grant us
> that we, being delivered from the hand of our enemies,
> might serve him without fear,
> in holiness and [right-doing] before him all the days of our
>   life. (vv. 68–75)

The theme in both passages is not consummation but deliverance—and correspondingly, not the hope for consummation but the hope for deliverance.

Let me elaborate just a bit on this distinction between deliverance and consummation. In *Eccentric Existence: A Theological Anthropology*,[3] my erstwhile colleague David Kelsey argues with great imagination and cogency that the story that Christian Scripture tells of how the Triune God relates to what is other than God has three distinct story lines: the story line of how God relates as creator and sustainer to what is other than God, the story line of how God relates as deliverer or redeemer to what is other than God, and the story line of how God relates as consummator to what is other than God.

Kelsey argues that though these three story lines interact, they are nonetheless independent of one another; none is a mere component or implication of another. To a person who has only heard of God as creator and sustainer, the news of redemption and consummation comes as *news—good* news. Redemption and consummation are not simply the outworking of the dynamics of creation. Likewise the story line of consummation does not imply that of redemption, nor vice versa. If God's creatures had acted as God wanted them to act, so that there was no need for the deliverance of which the One in the burning bush spoke nor for that which Zechariah expected, God might nonetheless have promised and effected consummation. Conversely, God might have redeemed us from the evils that haunt creation without offering us that consummation which is a *new* creation. Of course the story lines of consummation and redemption presuppose that there are beings who can be redeemed and whose existence can be consummated by a mode of existence that goes beyond what "the flesh" is capable of. But those story lines do not, as such, presuppose that the totality of what is other than God has been created by God.

What is it that God delivers us from? From affliction and from the suffering caused by affliction, says God to Moses. From our enemies, says Zechariah. Those whom God delivers are delivered from those who wrong them. God's deliverance is not confined to such deliverance; God also delivers us from suffering that is not caused by

3. David Kelsey, *Eccentric Existence: A Theological Anthropology* (Louisville: Westminster John Knox, 2009).

wrongdoing—"natural evils," as they are called. But the deliverance of which God spoke in the burning bush, and the deliverance that Zechariah expected, was deliverance from being wronged.

And more generally: the story line in the biblical narrative that tells of God's deliverance speaks centrally of God's delivering people from injustice. Thus there is no mystery as to why it is that in the redemptive story line of Scripture, God is over and over characterized as *just*, as *doing justice*, and as *loving justice*. The story line of the trinitarian God as deliverer and redeemer cannot even get going without the concepts of justice and injustice.

Return now to hope. The Christian hopes for two things: she hopes for redemption, and she hopes for consummation. She hopes for deliverance within this created order, especially deliverance from injustice, and she hopes for a transformed mode of existence that goes beyond God's work as creator and sustainer—a new creation, a new age, not brought about by the dynamics of creation. Two distinct hopes, neither to be assimilated to the other: hope for the just reign of God within this present creation, and hope for a new creation.

In the Gospel of Matthew we read that the last words spoken on earth by Jesus to his disciples began, "All authority in heaven and on earth has been given to me" (28:18). This theme, of all authority now belonging to Christ, is picked up at various points in the Pauline Letters, most extensively in 1 Corinthians 15. Let me quote:

> Christ has been raised from the dead, the first fruits of those who have fallen asleep. For as by a man came death, by a man has come also the resurrection of the dead. For as in Adam all die, so also in Christ shall all be made alive. But each in his own order: Christ the first fruits, then at his coming those who belong to Christ. Then comes the end, when he delivers the kingdom to God the Father after destroying every rule and every authority and power. For he must reign until he has put all his enemies under his feet. . . . When all things are subjected to him, then the Son himself will also be subjected to him who put all things under him, that God may be everything to every one. (vv. 20–28)

What does this mean, that upon his resurrection, all authority in heaven and earth has been given to Christ, to be retained by him until such time as he has defeated all competing rule, authority, and power, at which time he will deliver the kingship to the Father? What does it mean that Christ is now king and will remain king until he has fully pacified the realm?

A fully adequate answer to this question would require two lines of inquiry: an exegetical study of the line of thought in those New Testament passages where this proclamation of Christ as king comes to the surface, and a study of the Old Testament background to these passages so as to discern the connotations of "king" and "kingship." This is obviously not the place to develop adequately either of these approaches. I confine myself to a brief indication of the relevant Old Testament background.

The Old Testament writers were well acquainted with bad kings. What they had to say about bad kings is much less relevant to our purposes here, however, than what they had to say about good kings. The *locus classicus* is the opening of Psalm 72. I quote from the Jerusalem Bible:

> God, give your own justice to the king,
>> your own [doing of what is right] to the royal son,[4]
> so that he may rule your people rightly
>> and your poor with justice.
> Let the mountains and hills
>> bring a message of [shalom] for the people.[5]
> Uprightly he will defend the poorest,
> he will save the children of those in need,
>> and crush their oppressors. . . .
> All kings will do him homage,
>> all nations become his servants.
> He will free the poor man who calls to him,
>> and those who need help,

4. For "doing what is right," the Jerusalem Bible has "righteousness."
5. For "shalom," the Jerusalem Bible has "peace."

> he will have pity on the poor and feeble,
>   and save the lives of those in need;
> he will redeem their lives from exploitation and outrage,
>   their lives will be precious in his sight. (vv. 1–4, 11–14)

What comes through powerfully in this passage is that justice is the business of the good king. Flourishing (shalom) is also invoked. But the flourishing of the community is beyond the powers of the king to bring about; it will have to come from the favorable operations of the natural order, here symbolized as "the mountains and hills." And as to justice, the king's concern is not so much with the doing of justice as it is with the righting of injustice. The good king defends the impoverished, saves the children of those in need, frees the poor man, saves the lives of those in need, redeems their lives from exploitation and outrage.

Let's now go back to what Paul might mean when he says that all authority belongs to Christ until such time as all competing power and rule have been conquered, at which time Christ will hand over the kingship to God the Father. Given this Old Testament background, what else could he mean but that Christ is now at work in the world seeking to right injustice? Paul's implicit thought must be that there are two kinds of kingship: the kind that consists in the administration of a polity in which there is no injustice, and the kind that consists of struggling to right injustice. Christ's kingship is of the latter sort. When Christ's righting of injustice has been completed, that sort of kingship will no longer be needed, whereupon the Father will exercise the former kind.

It is often said that whereas most of humanity has thought in terms of a cyclical view of history, Judaism introduced a linear view. I cannot speak to whether there are linear views of history outside of Judaism and its sphere of influence. What does seem to me indubitably true is that Judaism employed a linear view of history—though not in the way that this claim is generally understood. In the Wisdom literature of the Old Testament, where there is little if anything of the story lines of redemption and consummation, only that of creation, there is also little if anything of a linear view of history. It is in the story lines of redemption and consummation that one finds a linear view of history—not because the biblical writers narrating these story lines had an ontology of time, but because the redemption and consummation story lines are inherently linear. They are stories of new things happening and yet to happen, not of the same old things happening yet again.

Fundamental to modernity is a blending and secularizing of the story lines of Scripture in such a way that there is thought to be good ground within the natural order for expecting that society will someday be liberated from injustice and we will all flourish until we die full of years. A few scientists have even speculated that a technology will eventually be discovered that halts aging, thereby eliminating death due to old age. Those who successfully dodge fatal accidents will retain the vigor, the agility, the curiosity, the libido, of a twenty-five-year-old.

This is optimism grounded in creation, not hope grounded in God. The claim or assumption is that there are grounds within the natural order for expecting this happy turn of events. Hope in the power of Christ to right injustice is replaced by optimism grounded in the powers of nature and humankind to secure both justice and flourishing.

Jean-François Lyotard's claim to fame was his announcement of the end of all grand metanarratives of progress. The announcement seems to me to have been premature. It's true that those narratives have died that located the ground for optimism in the potentials of central economic planning and nondemocratic political regimes; a vivid telling of the dashing of those hopes can be found in Jonathan Glover's *Humanity: A Moral History of the Twentieth Century*.[6] But the lesson drawn in most quarters of the West is not that we should give up on optimism but that our optimism should be grounded in the potentials for justice and well-being borne by a market economy combined with a democratic polity. This particular metanarrative, far from being dead, is flourishing as never before.

6. Jonathan Glover, *Humanity: A Moral History of the Twentieth Century* (New Haven: Yale University Press, 2000).

Christian writers and laypeople in the modern world have regularly succumbed to the temptation to jump on the bandwagon of one or another of the optimistic metanarratives of modernity, justifying the jump by saying that those particular dynamics of creation identified by the narrative in question are the *means* whereby Christ is bringing about his just rule. After all, God does use secondary causes, does he not? Some have thought that Marxism successfully identified those dynamics, others, that Nazism successfully did so; some have thought that American nationalism contained the crucial dynamics. Many now think that market capitalism combined with political democracy does so.

These conflations of Christian hope with secular optimism are one and all heretical. Though they all propose keeping God in the picture as the principal cause of those secondary causes that they identify, they nonetheless all conflate the story line of redemption with the story line of creation. Rather than redemption being seen as God's unexpected good news for a creation mysteriously haunted by wrongdoing, redemption is seen as the playing out of the potentials of creation. Let it be added that the currently popular metanarrative mentioned above is as implausible as all the others. Rather than expecting that market capitalism in combination with democracy will bring the end of injustice, should we not instead expect that the increasing integration of economies around the globe into one capitalist system will eventually result in a truly calamitous worldwide economic collapse?

If the hope that Christ will bring about his just kingdom is not to take the form of optimism concerning the potentials of one and another dynamic within creation, what form is it to take? Let me begin my answer with what will initially seem like a diversion. In an earlier chapter I mentioned the prayer service for the downfall of the government in South Africa organized by the leaders of the anti-apartheid movement. The service, titled "Prayer Service for the End to Unjust Rule," took place on June 15, 1985, and was attended by a large number of Christians. The prayers were of course addressed to God—not to the African National Congress, not to the South African government, but to God. The "Prayer of Petition" that the people together uttered on that day went as follows:

> This day, O God of mercy
> we bring before you all those
> who suffer in prison,
> who are oppressed,
> who mourn those who died in freedom struggles
>   in places like Soweto, Cross Roads, Uitenhage,
>   Sharpeville and many places not known to us.
> Deliver us from the chains of apartheid, bring us all
>   to the true liberty of the sons and daughters of God.
> Confound the ruthless, and grant us the power of your
>   kingdom.

In an open letter from prison—issued on March 23, 2001, and addressed to Kader Asmal, the Minister of Education in the South African government—Allan Boesak wrote as follows about the place of prayer within the protest movement:

Prayer is not doctrinal formulations or the mumbling of magical formulas. Neither is it an escape from our earthly responsibilities. Rather it is a call to take up those responsibilities, not on our own, but in total dependence on the grace of God and in the power of God.

Yes, for this very reason our prayers are sometimes political. They must be, because all the world is the Lord's, and there is no area of life, not a single inch, that is not subject to the lordship of Jesus Christ. So politics and politicians cannot consider themselves outside the demands of the gospel or outside the circle of prayer. We pray for politics, not because we feel much at home there, in that world of intrigue and compromise, of betrayal and awesome responsibility, but because even there we must assume our positions as believers. Even there we must dare to name God, to confess God within the womb of politics, and so challenge every idolatry that seeks to displace God in the lives of God's people. And so we came together to pray for transformation, political and societal and economic; and we prayed for personal transformation, for conversion, so that people might be driven by inner conviction rather than by political expediency.

We pray also because we believe passionately in the power of prayer. Prayer changes things, Christians say, and that is true. It is that conviction, you will remember, that inspired us in 1985 to call for a day of prayer for the downfall of the apartheid regime. We prayed then in the midst of a storm too, and we were viciously condemned by all who felt themselves threatened by a God who listens to the prayers of the oppressed. We were vilified by those whose interests could not abide the changes we were praying for. But the thing is, God heard our prayers, things changed, and apartheid is no more. . . .

[Christians] come together to pray because they are deeply convinced that transformation that is only social, economic and political, however indispensable, is not enough. They believe that we need the power of God in our lives so that transformation can be fundamental. Let me be bold, Minister: South Africa would not be free today if there were not such people, and South Africa needs them today more than ever before. As you reflect on the history of South Africa as you did last Wednesday, please do not forget this. More than anything, our struggle was sustained by prayer and faith. I know. I was there. Denying this historical truth will only exacerbate our already grave situation.

The occasion of Boesak's writing this letter was that two days before, on March 21, 2001, forty-five thousand Christians had gathered in the Newlands stadium in Cape Town to pray for peace, justice, and true reconciliation, while only about three hundred had shown up for an ANC rally at which Kader Asmal was the main speaker. In a fit of pique, Asmal attacked the assembly of Christians as exclusivist.

I submit that Christian hope for the righting of injustice will take the form, among other things, of prayer—prayer and song. It will take the form of petitionary prayer: it will pray in hope for the righting of injustice, not only for the righting of injustice in general but also for the righting of particular injustices. It will have the courage to name injustices, and then to pray for the righting of the injustices named. And if those named injustices are righted, Christian hope will then offer prayers of thanksgiving, not just for the righting of injustice in general, but for the righting of the named injustices.

What this presupposes, obviously, is the courage to identify the hand of God in history. To name the injustices for whose righting one thanks God in Christ is to identify the signs in history of Christ's liberating work.

In addition to taking the form of prayer, Christian hope for the righting of injustice takes the form of struggling for that same righting. *Ora et labora* ("pray and work") has always been the motto of the Christian church. Not just praying and then, in addition, working—praying for one thing and working for another—but working for the very same thing for which one prays. This presupposes, once again, naming the injustice. One cannot struggle for the righting of the injustice whose alleviation one has prayed for without naming it. The Christians of South Africa struggled for that for which they prayed; its name was the overthrow of the apartheid regime.

Many of us are extremely edgy when someone makes so bold as to identify the hand of God in history. With good reason: some of the things that have been identified as the doings of that hand are appalling. We don't have any particular problem naming some case of injustice and struggling for its righting. But we become nervous when people name that same injustice in their prayers and pray to Christ that he will crown with success their struggle to right injustice. And we become *extremely nervous* when, upon the success of their endeavors, they thank Christ for the righting of that named injustice. For how else is this to be interpreted, but as identifying the hand of Christ in history? To thank Christ for some named case of righting injustice presupposes, like it or not, identifying that as a sign of Christ's liberating work in history. And that makes us nervous.

Jacques Ellul concludes his book *The Politics of God and the Politics of Man* with an extraordinary chapter that he titles "Meditation on Inutility." "In spite of God's respect and love for man," says Ellul,

in spite of God's extreme humility in entering into man's project in order that man may finally enter into [God's] own design, in the long run one cannot but be seized by a profound sense of the inutility and vanity of human action. To what end is all this agitation, to what end these constant wars and states and empires, to what end the great march of the people of Israel, to what end the trivial daily round of the church, when in the long run the goal will inevitably be attained, when it is always ultimately God's will that is done, when the most basic thing of all is already achieved and already attained in Jesus Christ? One can understand the scandalized refusal of modern man who can neither accept the inutility of what he has done nor acquiesce in the overruling of his destiny.[7]

Ellul's point is clear. Christian hope for the righting of injustice is not an optimism grounded in the potentials of creation but hope grounded in the promise that Christ will bring about his just and holy kingdom. That hope is to take the form, in part, of our participation in Christ's cause by ourselves working for the righting of injustice. But then we learn that God moves in mysterious ways, sometimes bringing our best efforts to naught, sometimes wresting liberation out of appalling oppression. And that leads us to ask, what's the point of working in God's cause when God will bring about that cause in whatever way God pleases? What's the point of faithfully seeking to right injustice if our own efforts are overruled and the righting of the injustice emerges unexpectedly from the efforts of those who perpetrate injustice? Is it not futile to struggle for the righting of injustice?

Ellul's response—not so much an answer, I would say, as a response—is, "Just obey. No matter what, obey."

There is a divine law, which is a commandment, and which is addressed to us. Hence we have to fulfill it to the letter. We have to do all that is commanded. The sense or conviction of the utter futility of the work we do must not prevent us from doing it. The judgment of uselessness is no excuse for inaction. . . . Pronounced in advance, futility becomes

7. Jacques Ellul, *The Politics of God and the Politics of Man* (Grand Rapids: Eerdmans, 1972), 190.

justification of scorn of God and his word and work. It is after doing
what is commanded, when everything has been done in the sphere of
human decisions and means, when in terms of the relation to God every
effort has been made to know the will of God and to obey it, when in
the arena of life there has been full acceptance of all responsibilities
and interpretations and commitments and conflicts, it is then and
only then that the judgment takes on meaning: all this (that we have
to do) is useless; all this we cast from us to put it in thy hands, O Lord;
all this belongs no more to the human order but to the order of thy
kingdom. Thou mayest use this or that work to build up the kingdom
thou are preparing. In thy liberty thou mayest make as barren as the
fig-tree any of the works which we have undertaken to thy glory. This
is no longer our concern. It is no longer in our hands. What belongs
to our sphere we have done. Now, O Lord, we may set it aside, having
done all that was commanded.[8]

There is something profoundly right about this. Christian hope for
the righting of injustice takes the form of working for the righting
of injustice in the confidence that, in ways mysterious to us, Christ
will make use, for the coming of the rule of justice in his kingdom,
of what we have done along with that which others have done, good
and bad. But what I find missing in Ellul is the willingness to identify
the signs of Christ's redemptive work.

We do our work and then we say, "Make of it what you will, O
Lord." That implies that our prayers of petition and thanksgiving for
Christ's redemptive work of righting injustice must always remain
general; they can never name a particular injustice that we petition
Christ to remove; they can never name a particular injustice for whose
righting we give thanks. To discern whether this refusal to identify
the signs is acceptable, I think we must look at what Christians under
oppression who cried to God for deliverance have felt compelled to
do. The black and colored South African Christians found themselves
compelled not only to name the injustice that they petitioned God
to right but to name the injustice whose righting they thanked God

8. Ibid., 195–96.

for bringing about. To do that is to identify the signs of Christ's redemptive action.

The solution is not to refrain from identifying the signs of Christ's redemptive rule but to resist the arrogance of supposing that our identifications are indubitably correct and complete. Sometimes we miss the signs; sometimes what we took to be a sign proves not to be that. Likewise we must resist the arrogance of supposing that the signs of Christ's redemptive action coincide with the goals of our own successful endeavors. Sometimes what we achieved proves, to our deep disappointment, not to be very liberating at all; sometimes what seemed to be a failure proves to be surprisingly liberating. Christian hope for the righting of injustice is both confident as to its ground in Christ and humble as to our ability to discern the ways in which our endeavors contribute to the coming of Christ's rule of justice.

A good many of Rembrandt's paintings were initially painted by apprentices in his studio; Rembrandt then applied the finishing touches. Sometimes what a gifted apprentice handed over to the master was already so much like a Rembrandt that little remained for the master to do; on other occasions, though the preliminary painting came from the hand of the same gifted apprentice and was again very close to being a Rembrandt, it nonetheless fell short in such a way that the master had to do a lot of repainting in order to get it right. On other occasions, an apprentice proved so incompetent that Rembrandt had to do a major repainting in order to make it a Rembrandt. To everyone's surprise, however, it also happened on a few occasions that an incompetent apprentice somehow produced a painting that required only a bit of tweaking by the master to bring it up to standard.

The apprentices naturally hoped to produce paintings that would require very little repainting by the master; some even dared hope that some day the master would say, "It's right just as it is." But the master so regularly surprised the apprentices with what he did to their productions that they became rather tentative in their expectations as to what he would do. They did not entirely give up expectations; but by and large they just stood back and expected once again to be surprised. They did, of course, become rather good at discerning when the master had completed a painting and when a painting still needed his touch. The ability to recognize a true Rembrandt was, obviously, important for their work; how else could they aim at producing such paintings?

Some of the apprentices, observing that sometimes a quite bad effort on their part required just a bit of tweaking while at other times a rather good effort required major repainting, asked Rembrandt about the point of their work: what's the point of our undergoing all this training and our producing all these paintings if our best efforts sometimes require a lot of reworking and our worst efforts sometimes almost none?

Rembrandt would have none of it. Do your best to paint a Rembrandt, he insisted. I've been at this a long time; trust me. I would much rather have you try your best than have you slack off. What you do is important for my work. Trust me.

❖ 31 ❖

Recap

L et us briefly look back. We have discussed a number of abstract issues: the right order conception of justice versus the inherent rights conception, the nature of rights, the nature and grounding of human rights, the relation of love to justice. We have discussed a number of issues of biblical interpretation: the role of justice in the Old Testament and in the New, how the *dik*-stem words in the original Greek of the New Testament should be translated into English, what Paul says about the task and authority of the state in his Letter to the Romans. And we have reflected a bit on the structure of social justice movements. But the overall arc of our discussion has been a narrative: the narrative of what motivated me to think, speak, and write about justice in the first place and to think about it as I do. I mentioned that I would never have written this narrative had I not been prodded to do so by a number of people.

It was my face-to-face encounter with victims of social injustice— first, people of color in South Africa, a bit later, Palestinians, much later, Hondurans—that spurred me to think, speak, and write about justice and to think about it as I do. Early in my discussion I mentioned two ways in which starting from the wronged shaped how I think about justice.

First, starting from the wronged meant that I was never tempted to follow Rawls and the great bulk of his commentators in focusing on what would constitute a just distribution of rights and duties, benefits and burdens, by the basic social institutions in an ideal society. I was led instead to think about justice in our actual societies, societies that are far from ideal, societies in which people are systemically wronged. And I was led to develop an account that applied both to justice and injustice in our interpersonal relationships and to justice in the distribution of rights and duties, benefits and burdens, by our basic social institutions.

Second, starting from the wronged meant that, from the very beginning, I was led to think about justice along the lines of the inherent rights conception rather than the right order conception. It was not until a couple of decades after my initial encounter with the wronged in South Africa and the Middle East that I explicitly drew the distinction between these two ways of thinking about justice. But that initial encounter led me to sense intuitively that, at bottom, we do not have natural rights because they are bestowed on us by an objective standard of some sort but because of how we are. They are inherent in how we are.

Early in my discussion I drew the distinction between what I called *primary* justice and what I called *reactive* justice. The cry for justice by the people of color in South Africa was a cry for primary justice, as was the cry for justice by the Palestinians. I think it was because my reflections on justice were motivated and shaped by their cry that my subsequent reflections were focused on primary justice and not on reactive justice; the theory of justice that I developed was a theory of primary justice.

On my recent trip to Honduras I heard a cry for reactive justice. The wronged whom I met there were, of course, victims of primary injustice, some of it systemic, much of it episodic; but what they mainly spoke about was the near-total breakdown of the criminal

justice system in Honduras. The laws in Honduras are good laws, for
the most part; but they are often not enforced. Violators of the laws
are often not brought to justice. If rapists are allowed to walk about
freely, then not only will rape continue but their victims will be doubly
wronged: wronged by being violated, and wronged by the failure of
the criminal justice system to bring the wrongdoer to justice. Primary
justice is impossible in the absence of reactive justice.

There are other ways as well in which my way of thinking about
justice was shaped by starting from the wronged in South Africa and
the Middle East; it was not possible for me to explain those other
ways at the beginning, before I presented my theory of justice. Let
me do so now.

I have emphasized that running throughout discussions of justice
in the West is the distinction between the right order way of thinking
and the inherent rights way of thinking. Running throughout those
same discussions is another distinction that I would say is equally
fundamental, but to which I have not explicitly called attention. Let
me call this the distinction between the *Aristotelian* way of thinking
and the *Ulpian* way of thinking.

Justice for Aristotle consisted of fairness or equity in the distribution of benefits and burdens and in our exchanges with one another.
Justice is equality of treatment—with the understanding that the
equality of treatment that constitutes justice will often not be a flat
equality but an equality proportioned to relevant differences in the
recipients.[1] This way of thinking about justice has been dominant
in the West. John Rawls stands firmly in the Aristotelian tradition;
justice for Rawls is fairness in distributions.

The definition of justice that I quoted from Ulpian says nothing
about equality of treatment. To act justly, said Ulpian, is to render to
each what is his or her *ius*—that is, what is his or her right, his or her
due. To act justly is to render to each what she has a right to, what
is due her. The account of primary justice that I developed stands
solidly in the Ulpian rather than the Aristotelian tradition.

---

1. Aristotle's account of justice is to be found in book 5 of his *Nicomachean Ethics*.

Consider those people of color in South Africa who cried out for justice. They were, of course, victims of a gross maldistribution of benefits and burdens. But was that the root of the injustice that was being done to them? Suppose that the South African government, in order to achieve its ideal of separating the various nationalities in South Africa so that each could flourish in its own unique way, had undertaken to forcefully shuffle around the Afrikaners and English-speaking whites in roughly the same way that it forcefully shuffled around the so-called blacks and coloreds. Would this equality of treatment imply that everybody was then being treated justly? Of course not. It would mean that nobody was being rendered their right, that nobody was being rendered their due. It would mean that everybody was being treated unjustly. Starting from the wronged in South Africa and in the Middle East meant that it was the Ulpian way of thinking that drew me from the very beginning, not the Aristotelian. Had the wronged from whom I started simply been the victims of unfairness, I might well have been drawn to the Aristotelian way of thinking.

In the course of presenting my account of rights I noted that there was yet another way in which my thinking about justice was shaped by my encounter with the wronged in South Africa and the Middle East. I noted that the sort of accounts of natural rights that currently enjoy dominance in the philosophical literature are accounts that connect rights to autonomy: rights are protectors of autonomy. The autonomy of people of color in South Africa was, of course, severely restricted by the apartheid laws. But it never seemed to me that that was the root of what was wrong. What was wrong, at bottom, was that their dignity was being violated; they were being treated in a way that did not befit their dignity. From the very beginning I was drawn to a dignity-account of rights rather than to an autonomy-account.

The cry for primary justice by the people of color in South Africa and by the Palestinians had two dimensions: it was simultaneously a cry for the doing of primary justice and a cry for the righting of primary injustice. My thinking, speaking, and writing about justice have focused on the former. Had my mentality, training, and skills been those of a sociologist rather than those of a philosopher, it's likely that my response would have focused on the latter; I would have immersed myself in the history of these and other movements for the righting of primary injustice, and I would have developed a structural analysis of such movements, aimed at uncovering what it is that accounts for the success of some and the failure of others.

To the sociologist who suggested that I should write a sequel to my book *Justice: Rights and Wrongs*, in which I discussed how the perpetrators and defenders of social injustice could be brought to acknowledge the dignity of the oppressed, I should not have replied, as I did, that I would take his suggestion seriously; I should have replied that such a book would have to be written by someone who had the mentality, the training, and the skills of a sociologist such as himself. Perhaps the reason I did not make this reply is that academics all too often say, "Let somebody else do it."

Be that as it may, the challenge that he issued to me has continued to haunt me. Hence it is that in this essay I have taken some tentative steps, no doubt amateurish, in the direction of developing such a structural analysis. Some of the relevant questions have in fact preoccupied me from the very beginning. Why did my support for the civil rights movement in the United States, and my opposition to the Vietnam War, not move me to think seriously about justice in the way that my encounter with the people of color in South Africa and with the Palestinians moved me? And why was I moved to empathetic identification with the people of color at the conference in Potchefstroom who cried out for justice, whereas the Afrikaners who spoke up in defense of apartheid at the conference apparently felt no such empathetic identification?

Let me close with a question that writing this book has led me to ask myself. Would I be willing to extrapolate from my experience and say that there is something *right* in starting from the wronged in one's thinking about justice? My starting from the victims of social injustice whom I encountered led me to think about justice in ways that I regard as correct. Was that just happenstance? Might I have reached the same conclusions had I never stirred from my comfortable position as a professor of philosophy?

Let me state more precisely the question that intrigues me: Does injustice illuminate justice in a way that, for example, failures of love do not illuminate love? Perhaps the sort of existential confrontation with wrongs that I experienced is not necessary. But do wrongs illuminate rights?

Love comes in various forms: there is love as attraction, love as attachment, love as beneficence. In trying to understand one or another of these forms of love, there is little to be gained from looking at cases in which that form of love is absent. In his discussion of love as attraction (*eros*) in the *Symposium*, Plato pays no attention to cases of the absence of such love. Why would he?

Justice seems to me different in this respect. I do not fully understand why it seems different; but let me take a stab at identifying why it is. The main reason for the difference appears to me to be that mind and action bear a quite different relation to love than they do to justice.

To love something in the mode of attraction, one must be attracted to it and act accordingly; to love something in the mode of attachment, one must be attached to it and act accordingly; to love something in the mode of beneficence, one must desire its good and act accordingly. By contrast, treating someone as justice requires often has no telltale signs, either in the mind or the actions of the agent.

A provocative sentence in Adam Smith's *Theory of Moral Sentiments* goes like this: "We may often fulfill all the rules of justice by sitting still and doing nothing" (2.2.9). If you are walking on the Charlottesville Mall, I treat you as justice requires if I consider hindering you but refrain from doing so because I'm just too lazy to get up from my bench; I need not refrain from hindering you because I judge that justice requires that I refrain. But I also treat you as justice requires if the thought of hindering you never even crosses my mind. In both cases, the justice of how I am treating you is invisible. It has a certain abstractness about it. The observer of my actions sees me resting on my bench, nothing more; the reader of my mind discerns thoughts about other matters, nothing more. Yet in both cases I have treated you as justice requires.

The situation is very different if I wrong you by hindering you on your walk. Now I am actively doing something. My wronging of you is evident. It is this visibility of the wronging that brings to light what justice requires in this situation.

I think it is because, in many cases, treating someone as justice requires has no telltale signs in either mind or action, whereas the counterpart wronging does have telltale signs, that starting from the wronged illuminates justice. Breakdowns in justice provoke us to reflect on what it is that has broken down. Had the Afrikaners been treating the people of color in South Africa justly, the thought that they were doing so might well never have occurred to me. It might have passed me by. The injustice of what they were doing could not pass me by. I could not do other than start from the wronged.

So yes, a peculiarity of justice is that breakdowns in justice often illuminate justice in a way that breakdowns in love do not illuminate love. But not always. I have called attention to those cases in which inactivity on one's part constitutes treating the other person as justice requires; in such cases, the activity of wronging brings to light what justice requires. But there are plenty of other cases in which it is inactivity of a certain sort that wrongs the person. If I stand idly by while some thugs assault you on the mall and do not come to your aid, I wrong you; justice requires my trying to hinder them. In such cases it is injustice that leaves no telltale signs whereas justice is visible.

Index